Late Christmas present
from me to me.

D1485779

Suspended Sentences

Also by Jim Curran

Trango, the Nameless Tower
K2, Triumph and Tragedy

Suspended Sentences

FROM THE LIFE OF A CLIMBING CAMERAMAN

Jim Curran

Hodder & Stoughton
LONDON SYDNEY AUCKLAND TORONTO

British Library Cataloguing in Publication Data

Curran, Jim
  Suspended sentences.
  I. Title
  796.5022

ISBN 0-340-51817-0

Published by Hodder and Stoughton,
a division of Hodder and Stoughton Ltd,
Mill Road, Dunton Green, Sevenoaks, Kent TN13 2YA.
Editorial Office: 47 Bedford Square, London WC1B 3DP.

Photoset by Rowland Phototypesetting Ltd.
Bury St Edmunds, Suffolk
Printed in Great Britain by
Butler and Tanner Ltd, Frome and London

To all those many climbers who have found
themselves tied to one end of a rope with me
attached to the other, I offer this book.

Contents

	Author's Note	19
1	The Return	21
2	Furtive Days in Chiddingly Wood	23
3	An Epic on Lliwedd	31
4	A Great Effort	36
5	Mo, Joe and Trango	47
6	Barnaj II, Climbers Nil	63
7	Filming the Bat	73
8	An Invitation to China	83
9	Waiting for the Climbers	98
10	On the Rocks	110
11	What Took You So Long?	120
12	Don	134
13	Breaking the Habit of a Lifetime	143
14	B is for Bird, E is for Egg	159
15	The Edge of the World	170
16	To Be Continued . . .	176
	Index	185

COLOUR ILLUSTRATIONS
Between pages 96 and 97

View up the couloir to the Trango Tower
Mo Anthoine on the final hard chimneys[1]
The south summit of Barnaj II
Tony Riley leading an ice pitch on Barnaj II
Rab Carrington on the Bat[1]
Brian Hall filmed in mid-fall[1]
Our first view of Kongur
South Ridge of Kongur from the Pimple
The Old Man of Hoy[2]
Al Rouse on the first ascent of Act of Faith
Geoff Tier on the East Ridge of Palomani Tranca
Pre-Inca tombs, Lake Titicaca
Sea-cliff climbing on Lundy granite[3]
Henry Barber leads the Rasp
Pete Whillance and Ian McMullan on the first ascent of Conachair

CREDITS
[1] Tony Riley   [2] Neil Murison   [3] Pip Hopkinson
All other colour photographs by the author

MAPS

Asian Journey   13
The Cordillera Apolobamba   15

BLACK AND WHITE ILLUSTRATIONS

The author in the Calanques, 1974[1] 10
The author at K2 Base Camp, 1986[2] 17
Steve Durkin, my first climbing partner 27
Tony Riley, fellow film-maker 38
Before[1] and after[3] the drastic haircut 41
Al Harris[4] 49
Martin Boysen 54
Joe Brown 55
Mo Anthoine 61
Peter Boardman[5] 86
Joe Tasker[5] 87
David Wilson[6] 99
Mike Richardson 111
Bill Dark and the author on Bergercrack[7] 117
Paul Nunn 121
Phil Kershaw 133
Don Whillans arrives in Cornwall 135
Don on South Face Direct of Chair Ladder, 1980 136
Geoff Tier 145
Chris Bonington 167
Charlie Houston 181

CREDITS

[1] Paul Nunn   [4] Terry Tullis
[2] John Barry   [5] Chris Bonington
[3] Tony Riley   [6] Joe Tasker
[7] Ian Smith
All other black and white photographs by the author

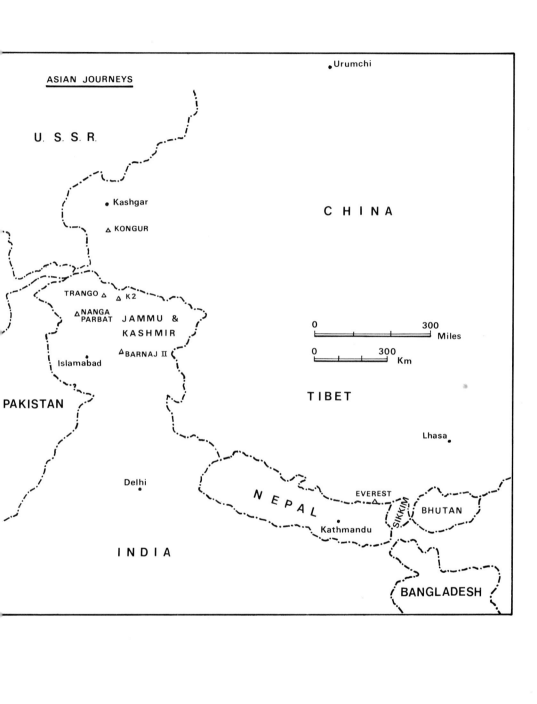

ASIAN JOURNEYS

U. S. S. R.

• Urumchi

CHINA

• Kashgar

△ KONGUR

TRANGO △   △ K2

△ NANGA
   PARBAT

JAMMU &
KASHMIR

△ BARNAJ II

• Islamabad

PAKISTAN

0   300
                        Miles

0   300
              Km

TIBET

Lhasa •

Delhi •

NEPAL

EVEREST
       △

SIKKIM

BHUTAN

Kathmandu •

INDIA

BANGLADESH

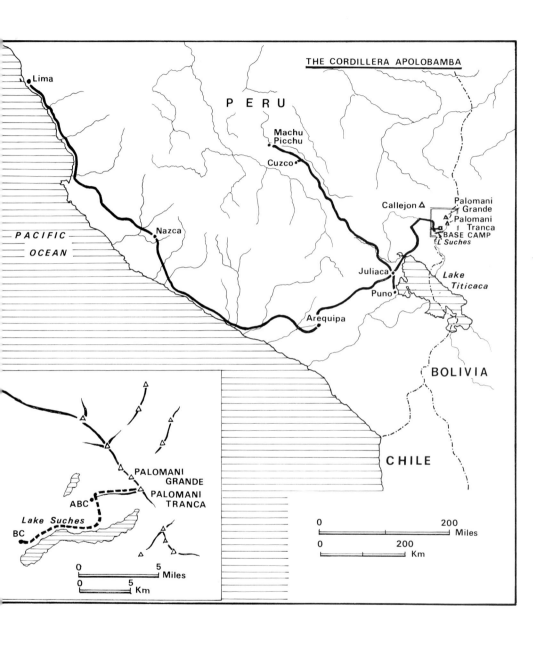

THE CORDILLERA APOLOBAMBA

P E R U

Lima

Machu
Picchu

Cuzco

Callejon △   Palomani
                     Grande
                   △ Palomani
                     Tranca
                   BASE CAMP
                   L Suches

PACIFIC
OCEAN

Nazca

Juliaca

Puno   Lake
              Titicaca

Arequipa

BOLIVIA

CHILE

0   200
⊢⊢⊢⊢⊢⊢⊢⊢⊢⊢⊢⊢⊢⊢⊢   Miles

0   200
⊢⊢⊢⊢⊢⊢⊢⊢⊢⊢⊢⊢   Km

PALOMANI
GRANDE
PALOMANI
TRANCA

ABC

Lake Suches

BC

0   5
⊢⊢⊢⊢⊢⊢⊢⊢⊢⊢   Miles
0   5
⊢⊢⊢⊢⊢⊢⊢⊢   Km

A CHRONOLOGY

1975   *A Great Effort*, an eighteen-minute documentary film on the life and poems and a climb of Menlove Edwards. BBC2.

1976   Expedition to Trango Towers, Pakistan. *Trango* film.

1977   Expedition to Barnaj, Kashmir, India. *Barnaj* film.

1978   First expedition to Choktoi, Pakistan.

1979   *The Bat*, award-winner at several film festivals, including Grand Prize at Telluride, Colorado in 1981. Second expedition to Barnaj (expedition leader).

1981   Expedition to Kongur, China, with Chris Bonington.

1982   *Kongur*, thirty-minute film shown at Christmas on ITV.

1986   To K2 with British Fullers K2 expedition.

1987   ITN cameraman on first ascent of Konachair, St Kilda. *K2, Triumph and Tragedy* published.

1988   HTV cameraman on North-East Ridge of Everest expedition.

1990   BBC2 cameraman on one of a six-part documentary series on mountaineering, filmed with Chris Bonington in the Karakoram.

A NOTE ON THE TITLE

It was first known as *The Slimmer's Guide to the Himalaya*. This title, coined originally by *High*'s editor Geoff Birtles, was around long before the book was written. Unfortunately it found little favour with The Powers That Be and I was gently persuaded to change it. 'What would happen if it ended up next to a pile of Jane Fonda books?' I was asked. 'Presumably it would be a bestseller,' I replied, but my logic went unheeded. *Cameraman on a Tight Rope* was suggested, instantly modified by a friend to the more accurate *Tight Cameraman on a Rope*. By this time *Cameraman on a Short Fuse* was even more appropriate. At last *Suspended Sentences* seemed a reasonable compromise. I hope however it does not end up in the Legal Affairs section or be seen as another Rumpole novel by John Mortimer.

Author's note

It is traditional to apologise on the first page of an autobiography for having the effrontery to regale the reader with 192 pages entirely devoted to the subject the author knows and loves the best. But this is not really an autobiography. It is a book about mountains and equally about people whose lives have been dominated by climbing them. For over thirty years I have been obsessed by mountains, climbing, filming and writing about their ridges and faces, glaciers and outcrops. From the scruffiest, disused quarry in Derbyshire to the lonely eminence of K2 there runs a constant, and some might say mildly unbalanced, enthusiasm. As well as the climbing the travelling to and from mountains has been almost as compulsive; strange places visited, vivid memories of absurd situations landed in or extricated from.

That climbing has largely been my *raison d'être* will, I hope, be obvious. So too will be the admission that I am far from being a superstar. I am, I suppose, a Boswell to the Dr Johnsons of the climbing world, a privileged observer, or as an unkind American reviewer once described me, 'a hanger-on in the British climbing pub scene'. From my humble position I have witnessed some of the great deeds of post-war British climbing – Joe Brown and Martin Boysen climbing on the Trango Tower, Pete Boardman and Joe Tasker on Kongur, Al Rouse on K2, Gerry Moffat winning the first Open Climbing Competition in Leeds, Chris Bonington and Pete Whillance exploring the huge cliffs of St Kilda in the Outer Hebrides – the list is a long one.

Throughout my chequered career as a climbing cameraman and film-maker I have made deep and enduring friendships within the climbing community. Perhaps by posing no threat to their prowess it has been easier for me to observe them, warts and all, in good times and bad.

It will quickly become apparent that I find much of what happens in the neurotic and self-obsessed little world of climbing very funny. I make no apologies. The climbing world has always been anarchic, frivolous and tolerant of all kinds of excesses. Its eccentricities and iconoclastic nature survives (but only just) in a dreary age of accountability, feasibility and mindless bureaucracy.

Occasionally humour and grief are close companions. I cannot ignore the fact that during the pursuit of the ephemeral joys of the mountains, so many close friends have died, not all as a direct result of climbing, but certainly through living their lives to the limit. Nick

Estcourt, Al Rouse, Mo Anthoine, Al Harris, Don Whillans, Pete Boardman and Joe Tasker are names that will frequently grace these pages. Their passing has caused me much grief and I have tried to recapture an echo of their spirit in this book.

I am sometimes quite surprised at how much I have climbed myself during the last thirty years, travelling through twenty-eight countries as well. If my summits have not included any 8000-metre peaks and my 'tick' list of rock climbs barely rises above Hard Very Severe, their variety and location more than compensate for their modest technical limitations.

It goes without saying that my thanks are due to all who feature in the book. I must also take this opportunity to write a few special words of appreciation to those whose contribution over many years has been as real but unmentioned in the text. My editor Margaret Body has, as usual, nursed, cajoled, criticised and encouraged me through its preparation. Rosie Smith and my daughter Gemma shared the typing chores. My brother Phil has given me constant support and advice which has been much appreciated, as have Geoff Birtles, Paul Nunn, Mike Richardson, Bob Burn and Tony Iveson. Since the first Trango Tower expedition Peter Lockey and Gordon Davison at Berghaus Limited have been incredibly generous and helpful in supplying their superb rucksacks that I have used and tested way beyond their normal specifications in carrying heavy camera equipment the length and breadth of the Himalaya. They have never let me down. Gil and David Gray of Javelin in Sheffield have also given their support, friendship and advice as well as their excellent fibre-pile and neoprene clothing. At Bristol Polytechnic my new course leader, Dick Le Feuvre, has been ever tolerant of my escapades and has taken (and forgotten) innumerable telephone messages. In Sheffield Pat Lewis of 'Mountain' has also been a real support. Ian Smith has produced so many excellent black and white prints over the years for me that I often forget that so many of them are from my own scruffy, ancient and ill-kept negatives. Similarly at Sheffield Photographic Ltd John Darwin and Jenny Thickett have been remarkably patient and generous with what must be one of their most ignorant and elusive customers. To all these and to anyone I may have forgotten I extend my most sincere thanks.

I

THE RETURN

THE OLD Fokker Friendship, twin engines straining and dissonant, nosed up through the dense grey layers of monsoon cloud yawing and bumping in the turbulence. Below, glimpses of wooded ridges, rocky hillsides and old dusty snow-fields began to emerge from the mists. I shifted awkwardly in my window seat, manoeuvring the big 16 mm Aaton movie camera to get the best view through the dirty yellowing Perspex window. Ahead I could just glimpse watery sunlight and the flash of high snows. Then the huge white bulk of Nanga Parbat drifted into vision. Even as I filmed I could feel the hairs on the back of my neck tingle with excitement. 'We're actually flying past the Diamir Face,' Chris Bonington, camera clicking, was enthusing to Sigi Hupfauer who had climbed the mountain in 1988 by the self-same Diamir Face and presumably didn't need to be told.

Opposite sat a weatherbeaten man who looked to be around sixty but who I knew was only a few days short of his seventy-seventh birthday. He peered at the ever-changing views with obvious emotion. 'I never thought I'd see these wonderful mountains again.' Dr Charles Houston was returning to the Karakoram. He had last made this flight, in the opposite direction, in 1953 following the epic tragedy on K2 when Art Gilkey had died. In 1986 I too had flown back from K2 gazing at the view with numbed senses trying to begin to grasp the enormity of what had just happened on the mountain when thirteen people had died in one of the worst Himalayan disasters ever. Like Charlie, I didn't imagine I would ever return. But now, four years later almost to the day, I was back in Pakistan, flying over the Karakoram Highway, recognising the bends and bridges in the road far below.

The plane skimmed past a rocky ridge and now, in brilliant sunshine, Haramosh and Rakaposhi were briefly framed in the viewfinder. As I started the camera again the view was suddenly blocked by the descending undercarriage and we seemed almost to fall out of the sky to land at Gilgit. We emerged blinking into the glare of the sunshine, to find ourselves surrounded by harsh rocky hillsides, groves of apricot and mulberry trees, tall poplars and brilliant green terraces fed by long and ingenious irrigation ditches. I couldn't stop grinning. I loved just being here, amongst these arid hills with all the sound and smells of the East around me. Even the immediate news that most of our film gear had been inexplicably unloaded from the plane just before we had taken off and left in Rawalpindi couldn't detract from the moment. I had come back to do what I wanted, to film and photograph the big mountains that have so dominated my life.

2

FURTIVE DAYS IN CHIDDINGLY WOOD

ONE MORNING in 1953 an event occurred that impressed me deeply. Then living in Ealing, west London, I was awakened by my father, who was normally the calmest and most restrained of men. 'Mount Everest has been climbed,' he announced, displaying an almost childish wonder that, being only ten years old myself, I found slightly embarrassing. *The Times* announcement – just the words 'Everest Climbed' – remains the first newspaper headline I can remember and for me the news completely eclipsed the other event of the day which was the coronation of Her Majesty Queen Elizabeth II. This I witnessed with no great enthusiasm at my friend Stephen Oliver's house across the road. His father was a doctor and they were the proud owners of a television, with a minute seven-inch screen. It had a bulbous magnifying glass suspended in front of it through which we watched, with increasing boredom, distorted chunks of the coronation service in Westminster Abbey. We reverted to playing cricket in the garden in the cool June drizzle.

Several months later St Benedict's Junior School assembled and, in crocodile formation, we all walked down to Ealing Broadway to the old Palladium cinema (now deceased) to watch *The Ascent of Everest*. This fired my imagination in a quite extraordinary way, though I never of course dreamed that thirty-five years later I would follow in the footsteps of men such as Tom Stobart or Captain Noel and film on Everest myself.

Everest took over from many childhood enthusiasms that had followed in quick succession, each one pursued with a single-minded obsessiveness that, I learned much later, had given my mother some cause for concern. These had included steam trains (inevitably), sharks, rhinoceroses (less obviously), octupi, giant squids (with frequent visits to the Natural History Museum), bagpipes (not related) and, most recently, volcanoes. In the entrance to the children's section of the Science Museum was an elaborate working model of Vesuvius, complete with backlit moving flames. In retrospect I now suspect that these may have been less than convincing to the adult eye. I was entranced and had made several unsuccessful attempts to reproduce the model in papier-mâché. However, the hour and a half in the Palladium was enough to consign volcanoes to the past, and I rapidly became a young Everest expert, devouring any book on the subject with avid interest. John Hunt's book was a family possession but it was Wilf Noyce's *South Col* that I remember more. Frequent visits to Ealing Public Library unearthed the history of the mountain and I became fascinated by the story of Mallory and Irvine.

The following year I went with old family friends to Cornwall. We stayed on a farm near Carbis Bay just east of St Ives. Apart from nearly drowning myself rescuing a beach ball, the highlight of the holiday was attempting a traverse over the rocks to the furthermost point of the bay. This, in the company of my two friends Richard and Mick Oswald, was never successfully completed. We were foiled by a 'mauvais pas' that I christened the Second Step, after the famous obstacle on the North-East Ridge of Everest. Recently on a visit to the sea-cliffs of West Penwith I revisited Carbis Bay out of curiosity and walked out to the furthermost rocks, thus finally finishing my first ever climb a mere thirty-five years later. Whatever the Second Step was in 1954, by 1989 it had become an easy day for an old man.

Inevitably, leaving school meant the end of organised sport. I had already become an enthusiastic cyclist. Together with a school friend, Robin Devenish, we had systematically explored most of the southern counties of England, and even youth-hostelled to Land's End and back in a memorable fortnight. Our parents, I now understand and appreciate, were amazingly tolerant and/or ignorant in giving us the freedom to go more or less wherever we wanted from such an early age. My father was a professional violinist with the Covent Garden orchestra. My younger brother Phil and I saw less of him than many children as his work at 'The Garden' kept him out on most evenings and rehearsals often took up Saturdays and even Sundays. When I was young I had been secretly convinced that he was a burglar, as he always left for work when it was dark, presumably carrying his violin case for the swag. He only ever banned two activities: motorcycling, for which I probably owe him my life, and playing the banjo. This instrument he refused to allow in the house at all, which was difficult as I went through a phase of playing traditional jazz when I started art school, and the offending instrument had to be swapped for a guitar whenever we rehearsed at home. I think the saxophone was also forbidden. When my purist upbringing refused to allow the instrument in the ensemble, the clarinet featured instead.

The cycling phase led almost inexorably to climbing. I first went to North Wales on a bicycle in the company of Mick Oswald, with whom I had shared the Cornish sea-level traverse years before. Staying at youth hostels in Llanberis, Capel Curig and Ogwen, we maintained our 100 per cent failure rate started in Cornwall by frightening ourselves out of climbing Tryfan and Snowdon in gales and heavy rain.

I was both frightened and hugely impressed by the wet Welsh mountains. Through the hissing rain and lowering cloud the glimpses of jagged ridges and grey featureless rock were wildly exciting. Like my first childhood views of the sea, I still get the same thrill, a heightened awareness of stark reality, whenever Tryfan's famous silhouette comes into view from the old A5 as you approach Llyn Ogwen. North Wales is the only place where I can recapture the intensity of those feelings – it was never quite the same in Scotland or the Alps. And for me the sight of the sea does nothing now, for reasons that will be apparent as these stories unfold.

It was to be another couple of years before I actually started climbing, and my first proper climb was in neither Wales nor Cornwall but Sussex in the company of another childhood friend, Steve Durkin. Steve was intense, shy, somewhat apologetic, ferociously determined, and at times single-minded to the point of lunacy. He had managed to get expelled from our school, St Benedict's, Ealing, by raising the Latin master's ancient green Raleigh bicycle up the flagpole on the roof of the main school building. This was an act of such outstanding initiative, ingenuity and not a little courage, that to this day I am bewildered as to why he was not rewarded rather than punished. It was Steve who persuaded me just before I left school to accompany him to Chiddingly Wood Rocks, situated in a highly private estate near East Grinstead. Our preference for Chiddingly Wood over the popular Harrisons Rocks I would like to think showed a certain independence of spirit that would grow into a highly developed urge to seek out the unknown, to push back the horizons and go where no man had gone before. Recently I questioned Steve who, more prosaically, reminded me that, as we had been sure we were about to make utter fools of ourselves, we had agreed it would be better to do it in private. I'm afraid he was quite right. We were and did.

Steve had already been to Harrisons and was the proud owner of a hemp climbing rope and a guidebook to rock climbing in south-east England. Here is its description of Chiddingly Wood: 'If there was ready access to these rocks . . . it is no exaggeration to say that this would be the finest outcrop in SE England, surpassing even Harrisons Rocks.' The crags, the guidebook pointed out, featured in R. Thurston Hopkins's *Ghosts over England*, which reports an interview with a local poacher. 'There's one thing I dare not do; I'd be afeared to walk through that girt valley below Big on Little [a famous boulder] after dark. It's a terrible ellynge place and a girt black ghost hound walks there o' nights . . . they call the hound Gytrack.'

I only retain a few impressions of that day in March 1959, but they are vivid ones. The wonderful, heady smell of sandstone, leaf mould, hemp rope and sweat; a grim struggle, plimsolls flapping, up one of the two or three easy climbs we managed on a tight top rope; furtive skulkings down rhododendron-lined paths with the bulging rounded buttresses like big beer guts poking through the undergrowth. A hermit's cave, with ancient lettering carved on the walls and a long dark walk to East Grinstead station to catch the last train back to Victoria. There, sitting looking out into the dark night and the lights of suburban Surrey as London drew closer, nursing aching arms and fingers, I felt the stirrings of a strange elation that thirty years on is as addictive as ever. Much later on we returned and bivouacked in the hermit's cave in the hope or dread of seeing the legendary Gytrack, which we didn't.

Robin Devenish was soon hooked, as was Michael Watkins, another school friend, and trips to Groombridge station and Harrisons Rocks were frequent. We travelled via Victoria on an ancient steam train we called the 'Spook Special'. Later, when Robin had passed his driving test he occasionally persuaded his father to lend us his Rover. This was a sedate green monster with lots of wooden interior design. We travelled down in style, rolling ponderously down the leafy Sussex lanes. The return, with clapped-out fingers, often needed the help of the passengers to operate the handbrake.

We were, I think, quite imaginative in choices of venue and visited many private crags, including another visit to Chiddingly Wood

Childhood friend and first climbing partner, Steve Durkin, seconds the final corner of Sceptre VS, High Rock, Cheddar.

when, under the protective camouflage of the eminently respectable Rover, we drove straight past the lodge guarding the road into the estate. On these youthful outings Robin and Steve were probably the better performers but none of us was particularly good. Occasionally we would watch in amazement a tall, rather arrogant climber, a couple of years older than us, who would nonchalantly solo the hardest routes around with no visible effort. His name was Martin Boysen. He radiated such an air of superiority I took an irrational dislike to him which many years later seemed quite absurd as he and his wife Maggie became close friends.

Our early days at Harrisons quickly progressed to North Wales, hitching up the M1 and then along the dreaded old A5, the hitch-hikers' graveyard. Each visit was made memorable by the journey as much as by the climbing which was fairly undistinguished. We were typical student novices, learning slowly, with a more than healthy respect for danger. In many ways my early years probably had more in common with pre-war university clubs. We were utterly in awe of any climb above Very Severe standard, and the then 'modern' climbs of Joe Brown and Don Whillans seemed to be from a different world.

In the days before the invention of the rock athlete, 'Eurocrags' and climbing walls we progressed sedately along the traditional paths of North Wales, a holiday in Skye, a few winter trips to Ben Nevis and then, rather more imaginatively, a holiday in the Pyrenees which proved to be far harder and more exciting training for the Alps than we had bargained for.

It wasn't until 1964, almost at the end of my time at art school, that I visited Chamonix. Like thousands of others, I became an instant devotee of Chamonix customs: Snells Field, the Biolay campsite, the Bar Nationale, the old Tunnel transport café. I was in there with the rest of them. The only problem was climbing. Again like many British novices I found the scale and seriousness of the Alps over-whelming and only managed a handful of climbs: retreating from almost as many and vowing after each minor epic never to climb again.

The highlight of the summer was an ascent of the Mer de Glace Face of the Grépon, a classic rock route on the Chamonix Aiguilles. In the company of a climber called Chris Oakley, a quiet, rather tight-lipped character whom I hardly knew and have never seen since, we walked round via Montenevers and up the Mer de Glace to the foot of the Grépon and climbed the first four hundred feet to the Tour Rouge Refuge, an ancient and half-ruined hut clinging to a ledge precariously weighted and wired down to stop it blowing away or falling off. It was about as sophisticated as a potting-shed.

Sleeping on its creaking wooden floor with alarming glimpses through the shattered floorboards to the glacier far below, I couldn't help feeling that we would have done better to stay in the Envers des Aiguilles hut, whose light we could see not all that far away shining alluringly in the last glimmers of dusk.

We slept badly, already tormented by thirst. There was no snow or melt-water near the hut and despite abseiling into a gully where the sound of falling water beckoned, I had found to my disgust that the rusty water-carrier that I'd taken from the hut leaked and by the time I climbed back it was empty. Next morning we climbed diagonally for several hundred feet before finding a patch of old snow to relieve our parched lips.

It was a perfect summer day with staggering views across to the Grandes Jorasses, the Géant and Mont Blanc itself.

Surrounded by mountains and perched halfway up an 800-metre rock face I felt a total elation. Somehow on the Grépon the fears and tension of the earlier routes abated and it was possible to revel in the position. This felt like the real thing; it looked like it as well and as the day wore on and we gained height I felt a bursting sense of pride just to be there.

Near the top the face became steeper and more compact. Being London-based climbers used to fingery wall climbing at Harrisons, we were ill-equipped for hand jamming up the granite cracks which I suppose were really quite straightforward. But at last we reached the base of the infamous Knubel Crack, the final pitch below the Grépon's twin rock summits. The guidebook had an intriguing description of how to surmount this obstacle with the aid of a jammed ice axe. Instructions were given move by move, like those on the back of a cornflakes packet to make a cardboard cut-out.

'. . . Now move L foot to Hold C and R arm to Hold D with R foot on jammed axe. At this point move L hand to foothold E . . .' etc, etc. Chris, who was a better climber than I, could make nothing of either the description or the crack and as time slipped by he slipped back down, cursing eloquently at his lack of literary and physical achievement. I was far too knackered to have a go myself and as the afternoon faded towards early evening, I began to get gripped again.

Annoyed at our failure on the last few metres, we traversed along a ledge system that led to the descent down the easy South-West Ridge, enjoying, as we did, the view down to Chamonix. Far below, the old Plage reflected a clear blue sky. The Plage was a muddy lake beloved

of English climbers who would crawl under wire fencing, like es-
capees from a concentration camp, rather than pay the entrance fee for
a swim. We started down and almost immediately ran into a large
team of French climbers, most of whom didn't know how to abseil.
What a place to learn, I thought, as we shepherded them slowly down
to the comparative safety of the Upper Nantillons Glacier. We had
wasted too much time. As we reached the Rognon, a rocky island that
marked the end of any real danger, it was already twilight. Stumbling
and cursing over the scree and with our tents, brews and food only a
mile or so away, we floundered around in pitch dark without a torch
between us. The French party, who were better equipped, had swept
past long ago. Around midnight and suffering bloody shins, but lucky
not to have broken legs, we settled down for a miserable bivouac. In
the Pyrenees the year before I had had a similar experience. Then I had
run out of cigarettes and spent half the night striking matches and
peering into my rucksack in the vain hope of finding the odd dog-end.
This time I had half a packet of Gauloises but – no matches. Although I
have not now smoked for five years, the memory of the frustration is
still almost tangible.

I now find it curious to recollect that after that holiday I felt as
though my climbing would be severely curtailed, or even stop
altogether. I was now almost a 'grown-up' and presumably would be
resigned to cleaning the car on Sunday mornings and reminiscing
about my not so very wild student days. Years later Nick Estcourt
told me exactly the same thoughts had occurred to him when he left
Cambridge University. I know now that I was hopelessly unaware of
how very deep the climbing bug had already bitten.

3

AN EPIC ON LLIWEDD

WHEN I left Ealing School of Art I opted for an art teacher's course in Manchester. It was near the Peak District and not too far from Wales and the Lakes. My first impressions of Derbyshire were of a strangely alien and harsh landscape that was not instantly likeable. The regular geometry of the rocks, the dominance of the horizontal moorland with huge skies and only the odd, abrupt, vertical nick of the gritstone edges, all seemed, to a southerner's eye, bleak and unforgiving. Consequently I tended to stick to tradition and go to Wales.

But Manchester was about a hundred times more interesting and enjoyable than I expected and soon marriage to Alison from Wilmslow and a flat in Didsbury were a natural progression. So much so that I have never considered a return to London. Art teaching, at first in schools but then part-time in colleges, left little time for climbing, but on one of Steve Durkin's infrequent visits we had a day out that gave us rather more than we had bargained for. Indirectly it led to the setting for my first film. On a cold Sunday morning in February we decided to drive over from Manchester to grab a climb in Wales. It was a clear, calm day and from Capel Curig the Snowdon Horseshoe stood black and impressive against a clear sky. Having come all this way we were reluctant to climb at Tremadog (the obvious choice on a cold day) and unwisely opted for a long old-fashioned classic on Lliwedd.

Lliwedd was the cliff beloved by the pioneers of Welsh climbing like Archer Thompson, Oskar Eckenstein, Geoffrey Winthrop Young and George Mallory. It is the biggest crag in Wales: a full 300 metres from bottom to top, and providing a wealth of very similar climbing in the easy and middle grades with only a few harder routes. But the climbing is quirky, often involving unprotected balance moves up flutings and shallow grooves where everything seems to slope the wrong way. It has few devotees these days, but still manages to give nasty surprises to those who underestimate its serious nature. As we were about to do.

There had been a light smattering of snow the previous night, but as we walked up to the foot of the cliff from the shores of Llyn Llydaw it was already melting and, we assumed, would scarcely affect the rock which seemed dry and almost clear already. We roped up at the foot of Avalanche, perhaps the most famous route on the crag. In 1907 it was described as 'the most exposed climb in England and Wales', though our guidebook dismissed it as being only Medium Very Difficult, 'a very open route of no special difficulty but of obvious charm'. I had climbed it before, along with the Red Wall Continuation and Long-land's Direct Finish. This gives one of the best day's easy climbing in Wales, if not Britain. It seemed well within our capabilities to do it again, even though we were starting at midday and it would be dark early.

The first pitches seemed reasonable, once we got into the style of climbing, but it was cold. Steve, chilled on the belays, followed slowly. As I led each pitch, patches of frozen snow, unseen from below, made an unwelcome appearance, even though they didn't affect the climbing. But as we approached the crux, a short awkward wall involving a step right round a steep little groove and out on to an exposed rib, the holds were not only brushed with powder snow but icy as well. I realised with a dull thud of alarm that we should probably have retreated already. But that was not so easy, for good belays on Lliwedd are few and far between, we had only one rope and the way down already seemed a long one. If I could get up this pitch, surely our troubles would be over? We needn't do the Red Wall pitches above and could simply finish up Terminal Arête, an easy, broken ridge leading to the top. After a nervous teetering struggle, my rock boots skidding on the polished verglas I rounded the rib. My heart sank further as I entered a world of white and grey with only the odd characteristically red rib of rock showing through. We had been deceived by the light snow shower which had effectively concealed almost full winter conditions higher up.

Committed, I found a perverse satisfaction in methodically making progress, labouring carefully from one rocky projection to the next, occasionally fiddling line runners round small spikes, but resigning myself to long, unprotected gaps in between. At the end of each pitch I had time to worry as Steve slowly approached. I stared down over the grey, flat waters of Llyn Llydaw and up at the Crib Goch Ridge beyond. Tiny dots traversed the famous Pinnacles. Lucky them, I thought, only an hour from Pen-y-Pass and the car park. Here Steve and I seemed to have suddenly been transported into a different world, and not one I had remotely bargained for when I had left Manchester suburbia that morning.

At last, in the late afternoon, I emerged on to the Great Terrace. In summer this is a series of broken grassy ledges, but now, to my slightly fevered imagination, it was more like the Second Ice Field on the North Face of the Eiger. I kicked steps in the hard, frozen snow, conscious that my smooth-soled rock boots gave little friction and thankful that Steve had produced a piton hammer with a spike from the depths of his rucksack. I made insecure progress to the foot of Terminal Arête which seemed from here to be a little more than a scramble to the top.

As twilight gave way to nightfall we climbed up the increasingly snow-encrusted ridge. It was technically much easier than below but with no gloves, inadequate clothing and no torch, I was rapidly running out of steam. After two or three pitches Steve, who had until now found the whole experience quite daunting, took over the lead for the first time. Suddenly the old determined Steve of schooldays came to the fore as he battled and scrabbled his way up the ridge. I followed, clumsily, up a never-ending series of pitches, shattered and numb with cold. After what seemed an eternity he pulled out on to the summit of the East Peak of Lliwedd. With relief I joined him and we coiled the frozen rope and set off down, skidding wildly on the hard-packed snow and ice of the descent path.

At first it seemed too good to be true: there was a bit of a moon and by its faint light we lost height quickly. But then we had to leave the ridge proper and traverse diagonally down to the left to regain the path back to Llyn Llydaw and our big boots. But where, oh where, did the path turn off? I knew if we missed it we could easily spend the night out on the huge broken hillside that led right down to the depths of the Gwynant valley. I knelt in the snow looking desperately for footprints. More by luck than good judgment I hit the exact point where the path left the ridge and, now out of the moonlight, we groped our way painfully slowly down towards the lake.

By a further miracle we found our big boots and with Steve now flagging I set off as quickly as possible towards the lake. Suddenly the sky was lit up by a flare and headlights appeared on the track coming up from Pen-y-Pass. Oh, Christ – a rescue. I tried to break into a shambling run. How humiliating – but of course our car would be the only one left in the car park.

At last I arrived breathless at the door of the Mountain Rescue Land-Rover. 'It's all right, we're safe.'

A curious face eyed me from the driver's seat. 'You might be, mate, but have a look up there behind you.'

I turned round and stared at the Snowdon Horseshoe. There were several pinpricks of torchlight up on the ridge, including one on the interminable slopes we had luckily avoided.

'There's at least twelve people reported missing so far – we'll be here most of the night.'

Steve caught me up and we walked down the Miners' Track back to the car with huge relief. Suffering slightly from exposure, it took most of the drive back to warm up. On the way I realised that two fingers of my left hand were still frozen.

Steve had to drive to London that night and I was back at work in Stockport on Monday morning, wondering, as I anxiously tried to rub some life into my still-numb fingers, whether the whole day had been a figment of my imagination. We had got ourselves into, and out of, a tight situation, in its own way far more serious than anything I had experienced in the Pyrenees, Alps or on the odd Scottish foray. We had ignored or broken many simple rules and, had things gone wrong, would only have had ourselves to blame. As it was, we had had a memorable day out and one that for many years became a personal yardstick upon which to measure subsequent ventures. 'At least it's not as bad as Lliwedd.'

After that unexpected reminder of a world I had been in danger of leaving behind, my year of part-time teaching built up to an absurd level in which I taught in five separate institutions in the same week. Clearly this could not continue and I applied successfully for a full-time lecturing job at Rotherham School of Arts and Crafts.

Eventually we moved across the Peak District to a new housing estate near Chapeltown, north of Sheffield. It was an unprepossessing semi, but cheap and reasonably convenient for Rotherham, some six miles away; it was also within walking distance of Wharncliffe Crags, an unfashionable, grimy gritstone edge blackened with the soot of the now defunct Sheffield to Manchester railway line running through the Don valley.

Knowing no one to climb with on a regular basis, I frequently soloed easy routes on Wharncliffe. Over a period of about two years I gradually grew to love the slightly melancholy setting and taught myself how to move with some degree of competence on the steep, rough rock. Slowly and painfully I learnt to hand jam, then with the heady zeal of the convert, realised that gritstone climbing was the best

I have ever experienced. It remains so to this day. Derbyshire, with its endless gritstone edges and limestone dales, is now the centre of my climbing life and I still get the same thrill of anticipation every time I drive out of Sheffield and up Ringinglow Road towards Stanage and Burbage Edges. The great skies and harsh moors seem to have mellowed over the years, and I now revel in exactly the same views I once found so disturbing. Countless summer evenings, climbing into the lengthening shadows, avoiding the midges and sharing the company of long-standing friendships have become so much a part of my life that I cannot begin to imagine ever living without them.

However, back in 1970 soon after the birth of Gemma in Sheffield, I was restless for a new teaching post and found one at the recently formed Bristol Polytechnic. Alison, Gemma and I moved down to the south-west of England wondering what would happen next. Twenty years later I am still wondering.

4

A GREAT EFFORT

WARM, WET west winds, the precarious, polished lime-
stone of the Avon Gorge and the elegance of Brunel's Suspension
Bridge; a feeling of mild decadence in Clifton's crumbling, over-
grown Georgian terraces and squares; middle-class students and a
pervading atmosphere of complacent superiority. These are some of
my earliest impressions of Bristol. Most of them have persisted to the
present day. But despite my early forebodings, many deep friendships
have grown and endured, even if two marriages have not. The
Foundation Course at Bristol Polytechnic has also survived, out-
witting a never-ending series of conspiracies to close it down. Now,
living for so long in an educational condemned cell, it has ceased to
bother me overmuch; the students remain stimulating, exasperating,
enthusiastic and lazy in about equal measures, and they probably feel
much the same about me. The day they go, I will as well.

When, entirely through my own fault, my first marriage broke
up, Alison, Gemma and our second child Becky went to live in
Altrincham, a pleasant middle-class suburb of south Manchester. By
an ironic coincidence in view of Alison's complete aversion to climbing, the children later attended the Bollin Primary School in nearby
Bowdon, and it was while waiting for them one gloomy afternoon
that I became aware of a vaguely familiar figure standing next to me. It
was Nick Estcourt whom I had met once before in Chamonix. His
children were in the same classes as mine. Nick, extrovert and
enthusiastic, was very definitely a known climber since the highly
publicised Annapurna South Face expedition and two Everest expeditions to follow. Nick was a stickler for good manners and, even
though I was a complete outsider, invited me to the local pub that he,
Dave Potts, Martin Boysen and Chris Bonington frequented. So out
of the blue I found myself admitted to the company of the Altrincham
All Stars as they were then labelled by the climbing community.

As far as I can remember I only actually climbed with Nick on a couple of occasions, but in the three years before his death on K2 in 1978 I saw far more of him than the others. We hit it off instantly and regaled each other with stories, jokes and legends of the climbing world. Nick, a computer programmer, revelled in the anarchic Welsh climbing scene and the outrageous behaviour of characters like Al Harris, Pete Minks and Mo Anthoine. He was, I suppose, a not untypical Cambridge graduate – outwardly responsible, conventional and conscious of his public-school background, but with a hankering for the freedom that climbing offered. Nick was into all the latest music and loved dancing and parties. Life seemed to speed up in his company. His slightly manic and highly strung temperament enabled him to live life to the full in several apparently contradictory ways. He enjoyed a turbulent relationship with Carolyn, his wife, who was a forceful personality in her own right. 'Everyone I know is terrified of you,' he once told her, 'including me.' Later, with my second wife Laraine, the four of us enjoyed a few memorable evenings. Perhaps because they were few and came just before Nick's departure for K2 in 1978, they have assumed inflated importance in my own mind but they have remained very clear. Like so many of his friends I was distraught by his death and even twelve years later find it hard to accept. But at least in his three children, Mathew, Tom and Martha, who are now themselves nearly grown up, it is possible to see traces of Nick, which is rather comforting.

By myself in Bristol I began to get frustrated with my own creative work. I had trained as a painter but my interests in climbing and mountains didn't seem to be easily translated into paint on canvas. I had taught myself the rudiments of photography but this seemed too easy. 'What about a film?' – a small thought turned around my brain. Me? Mechanically incompetent and technologically illiterate me? You (or rather I) must be joking. Why not? A film? I had occasionally used a Super 8 camera with the students on their field trips and had once filmed a friend, Chris Boulton, climbing at Wharncliffe. But could I plan and execute a whole film? In any case what would it be about?

In 1976 I applied for a year's secondment and in those far-off days of plenty I got it, a whole year learning to make films at Sheffield Polytechnic. It was here that I met Paul Nunn and Tony Riley who were, in their very different ways, to play such an important part in my life from then on.

Paul Nunn is one of the great institutions of British climbing. Irish-born and two days older than I, Paul was adopted by foster parents from Macclesfield on the edge of his home stamping ground, the Peak District. He has climbed extensively around Britain for over thirty

Tony Riley with whom I embarked on a course of joint self-enlightenment in the world of film-making.

years, adding innumerable hard new routes from the Cheddar Gorge in the south-west to Cape Wrath in the north, with plenty in between. Large, genial (he and I take up more than our fair share of space and volume in a pub), he has a mind that is often so many jumps ahead that his words are only the vaguest clue as to his real meaning. As a Principal Lecturer in Economic History at Sheffield Polytechnic, Paul practises the art of intrigue and political manoeuvre with a refinement that leaves me standing. He knows more about almost anything pertaining to climbing, Sheffield, agrarian policy in the late eighteenth century, economics, Buxton, yak herding in Tibet and who to visit on a wet weekend in Scotland than anyone else. In the Alps, Baffin Island, Russia and the Himalaya Paul's experience is vast. We have, over the years, collaborated on several projects and when I first met him I instantly felt a rapport that bridged our different backgrounds. One thing we do have in common however is our Catholic upbringing and education, still the source of some hilarity whenever the subject comes up, which is quite often.

Tony Riley shared a similar background to Paul. They went to the same school and started climbing together, though despite Tony's wide experience he never achieved the same high standard. He trained as a photographer in Manchester after dropping out of a course at Nottingham University. When I first knew him he had just started a job as a technician at Sheffield Poly. Tony is a complex character. He normally presents a rather dour, silent face to the world but underneath lies a deep vein of black humour. His background as a technical photographer makes him painstaking to the point of driving his colleagues to distraction, but his professional results are consistently high. It is fair to say that despite our collaboration on three films and our undoubted complementary abilities, Tony mistrusts my spontaneous hit and miss approach and I sometimes find his own systematic procedures rather stilted. But in our early days we worked very well together and I owe Tony a great debt of gratitude for our joint self-enlightenment in the world of film-making.

Still very vague about what the year would entail, I moved back to Sheffield. I wanted to make a film that showed climbing in a different light to the all-too-infrequent BBC Outside Broadcasts of the sixties and seventies. These, despite their enormous impact, tended to glorify the climbers and, despite deadpan assurances to the contrary from the stars like Joe Brown, Ian McNaught-Davis, Tom Patey, Peter Crew and occasionally Chris Bonington, the overall impression was one of superhuman courage and skill as the 'human flies' relentlessly 'conquered' the Old Man of Hoy or the sea-cliffs of Craig Gogarth. It seemed to me to be an interesting idea to make a film that dealt with failure rather than success. This may just have been an indication of my state of mind at the time, but at least gave me a rather different approach.

I had frequently enjoyed reading a classic article by John Menlove Edwards called 'A Great Effort', in which Edwards, the famous pioneer of Welsh rock climbing in the 1930s, described in great and often amusing detail a futile attempt to solo an anonymous rock climb somewhere in North Wales. The article had an intensity and perceptiveness that captured much of the pain and pleasure of climbing and it seemed (as it was a relatively short article) a good starting-point on which to base a year's work. I decided to recreate the event and to supplement the script with extracts from Edwards's poetry which, in its rather fragmentary, stark and tortured way, also spoke of unrequited love and great sadness. This former emotion, even though Menlove Edwards was homosexual, particularly appealed to me for upon my arrival in Sheffield I had fallen quite stupendously in love with a woman who did not feel the same way. Consequently the film became a kind of pleasurable penance in which all my romantic agonies were invested. It conspicuously failed to change the situation vis-à-vis the woman in question, but now that's neither here nor there. The moral must be that, in film-making at least, the end justifies the means.

Tony and I made several ventures to Wales to reconnoitre suitable locations to recreate 'A Great Effort'. Edwards was responsible for exploring the unfashionable cliffs of the thirties, like the Devil's Kitchen and, more important, the Llanberis Pass, but somehow neither of these fitted whatever it was I had in mind. Rereading the many draft proposals and treatments I made at the time I am amazed that the film ever got off the ground (literally and metaphorically) at all, so unrealistic were my earliest attempts. In the end I decided to revisit the scene of my own last 'great effort' and I went to Lliwedd where I climbed, with justifiable trepidation, Edwards's most famous route on the cliff – Central Gully Direct, a dauntingly loose Very Severe. This had been unrepeated for many years until Joe Brown did the second ascent in the early fifties. It still sported the remnants of an antique peg in its first steep section. Though this was by no means one of Edwards's best or hardest climbs, and certainly not the one referred to in the original article, it seemed to have exactly the qualities I was looking for.

From then I resolved the script and format of the film. As no one else would, I resolved to act out the part of Menlove Edwards in a series of still photographs which would be intercut with movie footage of me attempting to solo the same climb dressed as a present day climber. By cutting from past (still) to present (movie), I hoped to convey the timelessness of the original writing. It was a simple idea but it worked well. Once I had undergone the indignity of having my long hippy-style hair removed to a gruesome short back and sides (it must be remembered that around 1974 was the height of male hairiness), I bore a vague resemblance to Edwards. With an ancient sports jacket, tweed trousers and nailed boots the illusion was reasonably convincing.

On a gloomy autumn day and feeling an utter fool in my fancy dress, Tony and I walked up to Lliwedd and climbed the Sword, an Edwards Severe (which seemed a lot harder) that led to the lower reaches of Central Gully. Tony took over two hundred stills from which I made up a comprehensive story board as a guide to the filming. Unwittingly I had stumbled on an extremely efficient system that suited the painfully low budget perfectly, for in principle, if we

The author before his drastic haircut for the filming of 'A Great Effort' and, shorn, as Menlove Edwards.

only filmed 'in between' the series of still shots we would have the maximum usable footage for the minimum amount shot. Intercutting between still and movie should be made considerably easier with the stills already shot and edited. Though it didn't always work out exactly as planned we did have a lot more control over what we were doing than many first films, and we worked in the knowledge that each of us knew exactly what the other required.

The biggest hurdle was the shoot itself. I had a shrewd suspicion that, whereas promises of unpaid help on a climbing movie were offered from all sides, it would be best to assume that when it came to the crunch Tony and I would have to do it more or less on our own. And so it proved. But we would have to wait, first for my hair to grow, and second for the right weather, and it was February before we had a brilliant weather forecast from RAF Bawtry which predicted clear, cold weather in Snowdonia, freezing at night with good visibility. It was time to go.

Suffering the heady mixture of excitement, anticipation and acute anxiety that has become all too familiar at the outset of every shoot I have been involved in, we left for Wales. The next day saw us unloading the camera gear at Pen-y-Pass and carting it up to the foot of Lliwedd. As we would be working from dawn to dusk, we risked leaving all the expensive equipment unguarded overnight and saved ourselves the ordeal of carting monstrous loads back and forth.

As soon as we started filming everything began to click. Tony, despite his lack of film camera experience, was confident and assured and I, with no previous acting background, sensed what to do and we quickly developed an empathy that lasted throughout the week.

The first two days' shooting took us to the foot of the climb. There was every reason to film in chronological sequence, for each shot meant carrying the gear a bit nearer the cliff. On the third morning I psyched myself up to solo the Sword. Today it is graded VS 4c but its crux is at the start of the climb. Above is a long, easy arête that would give a classic open shot of a small figure silhouetted against the sky. This would be a contrast with the gloomy confines of the gully above. It was important that I got it right first time, both for my own state of mind and, even more important, because we were filming on a ludicrously tight shooting ratio that meant little or no film could be wasted on retakes. Not of course that I had the slightest intention of soloing the route twice! Once again it all worked well. With the adrenalin of being filmed I found the awkward start quite easy, and the long arête above was so enjoyable I could almost forget the consequences of a fall, and even that I was still being filmed.

At the end of this, the third day, we arrived at the bottom of Central Gully. It was here that we would need assistance, for Tony would have to film out on the left wall of the gully, from a hanging stance, while I would be stuck in the middle of the hard section of the route. Neither of us could do this without help and so two friends, Bob Dearman and Martin Barnicott, were employed to look after us on this, the crucial day.

Unbelievably for Wales, the weather remained brilliant as the forecast had predicted: cold and dry with staggeringly intense colour on the sunlit slopes of Crib Goch contrasting with the blue-grey North Face atmosphere of the cliff itself. As with my previous epic on Lliwedd there were frequent patches of old snow, but unlike that last time they provided only decorative backgrounds and the crag itself was bone dry, though very cold.

Up and away at first light, for we knew every hour of daylight would be needed, we retraced our steps to the foot of the cliff. The previous evening we had noticed two climbers who had spent hours on a route on the East Buttress were still several hundred feet from the top as we left the crag in the twilight. Now as dawn broke we were amazed to see them still short of the top, having undergone an involuntary and horribly cold bivouac. They seemed to be okay and we concentrated on rigging the stance on Central Gully for Tony. This involved a heinous crime. Bob Dearman, who in the sixties and early seventies was one of Derbyshire's best rock climbers, had acquired a reputation for using a lot of aid, which history later proved to be unnecessary. This, as with so many climbing controversies, was both inaccurate and unfair. Bob was responsible for many classic climbs that, as they have become more popular, have also become sounder and better protected. Occasionally, though, he probably was guilty of using a bit too much, but today was to be his moment of infamy. For Bob was about to place the first expansion bolt on Lliwedd! The most traditional cliff in Wales was to be violated by the bite of the drill and the smash of the hammer.

It was actually essential as Tony was to be suspended in the middle of a vertical, featureless wall and a bolt was the only way of keeping him in position: merely dangling him from a top rope would leave him slowly rotating in space and he needed to be as rigid as possible in order to handhold the camera steadily. And so the sacrilegious deed was done, with furtive giggles and an irrational fear that the ghost of Menlove Edwards would arrive to seek some frightful retribution.

After a lot of messing about it was almost midday before we were able to start filming. The crucial scenes described in 'A Great Effort' are all based around a few square feet of rocks as Edwards tried repeatedly to make a hard move and couldn't quite summon up the courage to do so. It is of course a feeling that every climber experiences at some time or other and the film would hinge on conveying the alternate feelings of hope and fear as I psyched myself up to act out the fateful moves. I was in fact held to the rock by a short sling attached to two nut belays out of sight of the camera, for below was the sweep of the lower reaches of the gully. Had I fallen off, I would have gone about 150 metres. I was very tense. This showed in the film but it was no mark of my acting ability for it was all too real. The filming once again went smoothly and as the afternoon shadows streaked across the lake below, and up the hillsides opposite, we knew we had got the film in the bag. The last shot was of me 'in extremis' rigging an abseil and retreating. Again it was done for real and was as frightening as it later looked. Tension at last relaxed as Tony descended from his lonely perch. Bob abseiled down behind him and removed the bolt with a remarkably light blow of the hammer, leaving a tiny scar in the vast acreage of Lliwedd's rock. Tired but totally fulfilled, we carried most of the gear down to Pen-y-Pass. It was over. Well, almost.

That night we celebrated. Too well, for the next day demanded some final long shots and the walk away from the crag. Poor Tony was so hung-over he was barely able to walk up the Miners' Track and the weather had at last broken. Swathes of mist drifted around Lliwedd's twin peaks and the last shots of the film are every bit as sad-looking as the final narration requires. With beginners' luck we had cracked it.

At least we thought we had. Of course we had only completed the tip of the iceberg. During my time in Sheffield I had worked with other full-time students on the film course, acting as cameraman, sound recordist and general dogsbody on several films. However, the mysteries of editing picture and narration were still a closed book to me. Although the rushes of the film seemed encouraging I had very little idea of how to start editing. But it was in the studios back in Sheffield that I became hooked for ever on film-making. For under the tolerant guidance and good humour of lecturers Barry Callaghan and Paul Heywood I discovered that putting film together was not just enjoyable, though incredibly time-consuming – it was the most exciting, creative work I had ever been involved with. The satisfaction of making a scene work and the gradual addition of layers of illusion in the form of voice and sound effects was an addictive and quite wonderful new world to explore and one that completely eclipsed my lifelong passion for painting.

To the layman it must often seem that climbing films are, to a greater or lesser extent, a cheat. 'Of course you must tilt the camera', 'I bet the ground is only just out of sight', 'You do it all with a telephoto lens.' There is a grain of truth in all these assertions and certainly in all-action films made for the commercial cinema there are, literally, no holds barred.

I hope I can say that in all the films I have ever been involved with that little, if anything, has ever been 'rigged' to make it look more spectacular than it actually was. Occasionally, as in shooting *The Bat* several years later, we minimised the dangers of a long fall by judicious use of concealed protection and a full body harness, but the fall itself was all too real. The drama, suspense and fear are almost all created in the editing process. Juxtaposing images, pacing the shots, and in particular the use of music and sound effects can dramatically change an audience's perception of what they think they are watching. To that extent film is a highly manipulative medium, but I have always tried to ensure that what is shown on the screen is as straight-forward and as honest as possible.

There is, of course, a big difference between a dramatised recreation like *A Great Effort*, and an expedition film which is, or should strive to be, an objective documentary. Whether on Trango or Kongur or K2 many years later, I have always tried to stick to the principle that the story and the footage are both describing the same thing. It is inevitable, however, that the story will be a simplification. An event that lasts two months has to be compressed into a mere twenty-six or fifty-two minutes. Clearly the film can only be a cameo of what actually happened and the film-maker has a heavy responsibility to recapture the essence of the expedition and to highlight the critical moments. This is not too difficult if the expedition is happy and successful, and for many years I kidded myself that I would be able to deal with whatever happened without any fear of bias or emotional involvement. However the complex and traumatic events on K2 in 1986 made me face up to the problems that beset all film-makers when dealing with highly charged matters of life and death, and I came to realise the hard way that film is such a sensitive and subtle medium that it is almost impossible to control completely its many layers of meaning and response. In many ways writing is more straightforward and allows in-depth analysis of more than one or two issues. Largely as a result of the K2 film, I have become less interested in expedition documentaries. My first film love, the dramatised documentary, seems to be a more worthwhile format to pursue in the future.

Slowly *A Great Effort* took shape, and I became increasingly neur-otic about how the finished product would be received. I thought and hoped it would be passable, perhaps even quite good, but I had absolutely nothing to compare it with. I wondered if I was going to make a complete fool of myself as it got nearer and nearer to completion. My brother Phil had written and performed piano music specially for the film and his sensitive and evocative pieces, timed to the second, put the finishing touches on the mood. Only one final task was necessary. Tony and I would neg cut the film ourselves. This is a job of mind-blowing tedium and precision, as every frame of edited footage has to be matched with precisely the same negative film, assembled in the correct order for the final print. It is a job that is normally done by specialists but we couldn't afford that luxury. As soon as we started I regretted what we had taken on. Two days of solid misery seemed likely to give us nervous breakdowns but at last it was finished and the rolls of negative sent off for the answer print. I think on this first film I was more excited and worried than I had ever been before or since, as I drove down to Sheffield Midland station to pick up the small film can that represented a year's work. Hardly daring to watch, we projected it in college in an empty viewing studio. It was an almost perfect print and, in the euphoria that followed, I knew beyond doubt that this, more than anything, was what I wanted to do again and again. Above all, my fantasy of one day going to the Himalaya had moved a small step nearer to reality.

5

MO, JOE AND TRANGO

BEFORE AND during the making of *A Great Effort*, I met and gradually got to know Mo Anthoine and his wife Jackie. They lived in a cottage, slowly being renovated, in Nant Peris at the foot of the Llanberis Pass. Mo ran Snowdon Mouldings, a factory making the famous Joe Brown helmets and Curver ice axes. Later the company expanded to manufacture tents and clothing. This side of the company was run by Jackie. Mo was without doubt the funniest person I have ever met. For fifteen years I had the pleasure of his company, his endless banter, sense of the absurd, ridiculous analogies, black humour and occasional outrageous behaviour.

Mo was very definitely his own man. Despite being one of Britain's most experienced members of the loose-knit group of climbers regularly employed for film and television work, Mo remained firmly behind the camera and the general public had little exposure to his biting wit. A pity, for Mo could easily have become a media personality in his own right, but Mo never sought that kind of existence. He had in any case a vast circle of friends that cut across every social stratum. His iconoclastic nature, that could easily have offended conventional mortals, invariably had the reverse effect, for Mo, even at his most outspoken, had the ability to charm the hind legs off a donkey. Even my mother, who once listened to a tape-recording of one of his more lurid stories, was reduced to hysterical giggles after the first utter horror at his inventive language had worn off. She only met him once, on the occasion of my second marriage, but became, like so many others, an instant fan.

It is quite impossible to capture Mo's style in print. On top of that the vast majority of 'Moisms' are simply lost, as they were invariably told while both narrator and audience were well on the way to alcoholic amnesia. Mo was at his best in a pub. Invariably it was the Padarn Lake in Llanberis (later the venue was the Victoria Hotel) where on Friday and Saturday nights Mo held court to the ever-changing company for whom seeing Mo was one of the main ingredients of a good Welsh weekend.

Though Mo dominated proceedings, Jackie gave nearly as good value. One night in the Padarn she overdid the gin and tonics and was violently sick after the pub, though next morning she showed no ill effects. She bustled noisily round cooking breakfasts for Mo and me, both decidedly jaded ourselves.

'God, Jackie, you were pissed last night,' I muttered into my coffee.

'Me? Pissed? I was not.' Jackie was quite offended at the thought.

'Not pissed?' Mo looked up. 'Jackie,' he explained patiently, 'you were doing handstands on the bar in the Padarn with no knickers on, shouting "Use me as an eggcup." I was selling ostrich eggs,' he added, as if to jog her memory.

Mo was one of the most experienced and widely travelled ex-peditioners in Britain, though without anything like the high public profile of climbers like Chris Bonington or Doug Scott. In the early seventies trips to Peru, Patagonia and Nepal were not taken quite as much for granted as they are today. Mo's were largely self-financed and undertaken in the company of close friends to whom, over the years, Mo showed unswerving loyalty and never-ending generosity. His wanderlust had in fact started early when, in the company of Fox (Ian Cartlege, known to all as Fox for reasons that are obvious when you meet him), Mo hitched to Australia. The tales recounted from the journey have taken on an almost epic quality: the New Year's Eve in Melbourne for instance when Mo, already speechlessly drunk, gatecrashed a party. 'Are you the drummer?' 'Yes,' lied Mo confidently. It took less than a minute before his subterfuge was discovered and in the ensuing fracas a Welsh dresser to which Mo had become attached was demolished. The double bass player took pity on him and drove him home in his Volkswagon Beetle. When Mo got out he managed to put his foot through the bass, wedged across the back seat. A fight ensued that woke up a neighbour who came to investigate in his pyjamas, had a heart attack and died. Mo's telling of the story took at least twenty minutes.

Though weekends with Mo involved a high profile in the pub, he could occasionally be persuaded to climb a more than respectable standard before the serious business of the day. Frequently Saturday evening would end up at a party. Even more frequently it was with that other bastion of Llanberis high life, Al Harris.

Al Harris, the climbing world's answer to Mick Jagger.

I had first met Al many years earlier when he landed on my head at High Rocks Annexe near Tunbridge Wells. ''Allo, I'm Al,' said an unmistakably south London voice. He was about sixteen at the time and we quickly adjourned to the High Rock Inn for the first of what would be eventually several hundred pints. 'Harris' as he was often more simply known, never really seemed to grow any older. His objective in life was to play full-time and he managed it reasonably well through the sixties and seventies, which was no mean feat. Al was a brilliant, if erratic, rock climber and the ringmaster, clown and trapeze artist of the Welsh climbing fraternity. For fifteen years he masterminded virtually all the entertainment that Llanberis had to offer. Whatever you thought of him, he was a pivotal figure in many climbers' lives. True, it was a scene of alcohol and soft drugs, of petty shoplifting and occasional run-ins with the law. But Al's zest for life somehow overrode all the social transgressions. Between Al's house in Deiniolen and Mo's in Nant Peris, there existed a social scene that ran from quite respectable to pretty decadent. I found that so long as climbing played some part in it all, I could enjoy most of it but, on its own, the decadent end was hard to sustain for any length of time. I must admit, however, that I did give it a good try on many occasions.

Knowing Mo did not mean that Tony and I had any right to go with him on one of his expeditions. But to my surprise *A Great Effort* was televised on BBC2's *First Picture Show* in 1975 and reasonably well received. In the same year Mo, Joe Brown, Ian McNaught-Davis, Bill Barker, Dave Potts and Martin Boysen had mounted a small expedition to the highly sought-after Trango Tower in the Karakoram. The expedition had failed in dramatic circumstances when Martin managed to trap his knee in an overhanging crack some two-thirds up the 6250-metre granite spire. He had eventually freed himself, but the expedition, extended and short of time and manpower, had been abandoned. Mo, with his normal incorrigible optimism, wanted to go back in 1976 to finish what he was fairly convinced were the three pitches that remained between the knee-jam crack and the summit. Tony and I persuaded Mo that our presence to make a film would be a good idea.

By the mid-1970s the Trango Towers had, for many climbers, acquired an almost mystical significance. Years earlier, I had bought a battered paperback edition of Eric Shipton's *Upon That Mountain* which had a black and white photograph entitled 'Unnamed peak above the Trango Glacier'. This proved to be Uli Biaho, and not actually one of the Trango Towers at all, though in the hardback version was another tantalising picture 'Unclimbed Shaksgam granite peak'. This, in fact, was the Trango, or Nameless Tower. It was almost certainly the word itself that turned me on: Trango *sounded* wildly remote and highly romantic. In Joe Brown's autobiography, *The Hard Years*, he mentioned the Trango Tower as an unfulfilled objective and had named a climb in North Wales after it. It came as something of an anticlimax quite recently to find out that 'Trango' in all probability means 'sheep pen' and is presumably the name of a patch of grazing land next to the glacier which carries the same name. Perhaps I shouldn't have revealed that.

It is now thirteen years since the Trango expedition. It still remains the best, most memorable and happiest adventure of my life. Climbing styles and attitudes have changed a lot in thirteen years, but our expedition was a small but significant step forward in purely technical terms. The mystery surrounding most of the Karakoram and Tibetan mountains has all but disappeared now and while I have no doubt that each generation will discover its own challenges in the Himalaya, simply exploring places for the first time will, I fear, not feature very highly.

For twenty years, until 1975, the Karakoram in northern Pakistan was closed to expeditions. When it opened, many of the world's most attractive mountains were suddenly available to climb (at a price). Many, like the Trango Towers, were unclimbed and had never even been attempted. But Mo's expedition failed, not just because of Martin's knee, but because of the chaotic organisation, lack of porters, strikes and go-slows that left the team with less than three weeks on the mountain. In 1976 Mo, wise to the possible delays and, as usual, learning quickly from experience, was more organised. He and Tony Riley left in early May in Mo's old Transit van for the drive to Pakistan. In those halcyon days before Iran and Afghanistan both became enmeshed in their own very different troubles, it made sense to take the expedition equipment, if not all the members, overland. It was an adventure in its own right and one that I was to share on the return journey and then participate in more fully on another expedition the following year.

But this time I flew out from Heathrow: the first of what were to be many departures to the East in the company of star climbers in whose ranks I felt, deep down, hopelessly out of place. Joe Brown and Martin Boysen had both dominated the British climbing scene for so long it was hard not to be overawed, like the legendary schoolboy in the crowd, asked to play in a first division football match. I dreaded the thought of making a fool of myself, yet knew it was an opportunity that I couldn't turn down.

We took with us primitive film gear loaned from both Bristol and Sheffield Polytechnics. It is one of the very few major regrets in my life, however, that both the gear and our own inexperience let us down. If I could do it again I am sure that *Trango* would be one of the best climbing films ever made. But we started on a difficult and daunting mountain. Tony in particular performed marvels in getting as high as he did with substandard cameras and old film stock that were not really suitable for the demands of high-altitude shooting. We certainly learned from experience but I wish it had been on something rather more amenable, and that Trango had happened a year or so later.

Almost as soon as I arrived in Pakistan I became hooked on expedition life. It is hard to explain the attraction to those who see expeditions as no more than a gruelling, uncomfortable and dangerous waste of time (and those include many climbers who only go once). For they are indeed all these things, and more. But they are also times of profound happiness in simply existing in an alien, beautiful, yet often hostile environment; of travelling in new places where your senses are heightened by new sights, sounds, tastes and smells. They are times when goals are simple (and often attainable), where the criteria of success and failure are easy to understand, and where real friendships can be developed and tested to the full.

Unlike the first Trango expedition, when from a very early stage the expedition had been ruined by porter strikes, our walk-in, up the Braldu Gorge via Askole and across the Biafo Glacier towards the Lower Baltoro, was a pleasure. I know it was also hard work but now the predominant memory is of high good humour all the way, with Mo unstoppable in his never-ending ability to reduce each of us to hysterics. I also remember with considerable nostalgia the pungent smell of juniper, the woodsmoke of the porter fires as they cooked their coarse chappatis, the combination of water noise from the roaring Braldu and the characteristic high-pitched whistle of porters adjusting their loads, the cry of the local Muslims in morning prayer as they knelt to the West, to Mecca, the all-pervading dust that covered us and everything else in the Karakoram, and the fantastic ever-changing panoramas of gothic rock architecture whose form and scale became progressively more impressive as we slowly approached our journey's end.

The Trango Towers are the first group of granite spires that flank the great thirty-seven-mile Baltoro Glacier that flows from Concordia to Paiju, a green and fertile campsite two miles from its snout. In fact to get to our own mountain we avoided going on the Baltoro at all.

We skirted its snout by a devious path that led up and across the much smaller Uli Biaho Glacier and then to the Trango Glacier that flows into the Baltoro. From here a short day led to the foot of the Trango Tower itself. The weather had been mediocre for the latter half of the walk-in with only tantalising glimpses of the soaring granite walls around us. Suddenly as I plodded slowly up the lateral moraine of the glacier I was aware of a wide couloir on my right. I looked up, and there it was. To this day it remains the single most dramatic mountain I have ever seen. True, the first view of K2, for instance, is more imposing, and Everest has immense grandeur and charisma, but for sheer reeling, breathtaking verticality, Trango Tower is matchless. It is in reality so much more slender and steep than most photographs show. It also, curiously, leans slightly to the left, but in almost all our slides we subconsciously corrected this. My profound doubts as to my presence on this mountain in that company surfaced once more as I realised that I was about to embark on something far more serious and frightening than anything I had done before. The thought of swinging around filming on fixed ropes on vertical or overhanging rock above thousands of feet of space was enough to give me mild nausea. Just looking up the 2500 or so metres between me and the summit of the Tower was really quite enough for me to be going on with.

But first we had to establish our Base Camp at the foot of the couloir and pay off most of the thirty-odd Balti porters who had carried our gear this far. We kept eight on to carry up to an Advance Base at the foot of the Tower itself. The previous year this had not happened and the team had had the gruelling experience of making several heavy carries up the interminable scree-filled gully. This had cost much time and energy that hopefully would be considerably eased this year.

For me the memories of Trango are of extreme effort to keep going. I was frankly frightened of my ability to acclimatise successfully. I have always done so very slowly but, touch wood, without any really serious problems. But this was the first time I had been higher than 3000 metres and I was very conscious of the dangers of altitude. Eight expeditions later I am sure I was right to be worried. I have seen many mild cases of high-altitude sickness, both cerebral and pulmonary, and one severe instance which mercifully was not fatal. I have never helped my own performance by being fat and unfit before expeditions (which seems to be my natural state) but I am still dubious as to just how much this affects performance in an activity that takes months rather than days. Mo had lulled me into a false state of security before we left Britain with his reassurance that heavy physical exercise was a waste

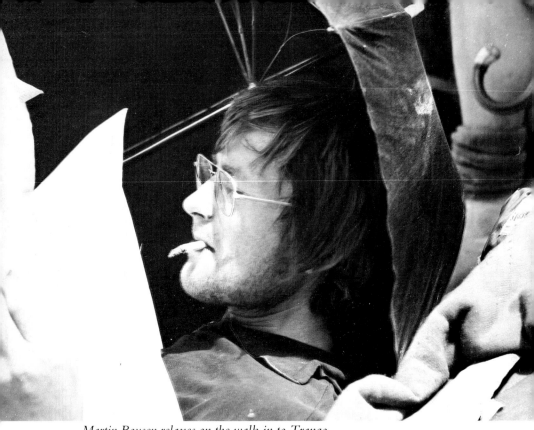

Martin Boysen relaxes on the walk-in to Trango.

of time and that the walk-in and inevitable stomach upsets would more than compensate for initial corpulence. 'The best thing you can do is sit in a warm oven eating shit sandwiches,' was his cryptic comment, summing up pre-expedition training in one sentence.

Despite my inadequacies, I was already deriving immense pleasure from the varied company of the whole team. Martin Boysen, a year or so older than I, was generally laid back, amusing and considerate in his awareness that Tony and I were finding everything hard work. He is, however, prone to occasional fits of frightful bad temper and what Mike Thompson once referred to as his 'legendary patience' was often stretched to its not very flexible limits. The stroppy schoolboy I was so in awe of many years ago had become a slightly eccentric school teacher, studiedly casual, eternally scruffy and quite wonderfully absent-minded. He has however retained an awe-inspiring contempt for fools of all kinds. Martin's dismissive comments are not to be on the receiving end of, although sometimes his mocking wrath can be self-defeating. On one occasion, bouldering on Stanage with Rab Carrington and Al Rouse, he tired of the eternal list of status routes claimed by Al in particular, whose capacity for advanced bullshitting was legendary. Eventually Martin exploded. 'You needn't try to impress me – I've been climbing here for over thirty years and I *still*

Joe Brown, the Old Master.

only know the names of two routes – one's Quietus and the other's
. . . well, I can't actually bloody well remember the name of the
other . . .' Not long after, Martin and Rab were listening to the self-
denigrations of an unknown climber failing on a route.

'I just can't understand it,' bemoaned the hapless leader as he
shamelessly rested on a tight rope, 'I could piss up this last year and I
can't even begin to do it now – I just can't understand why.'

'It's because you're no fucking good, that's why.' Martin's scorn
was consummate.

If Martin was generally laid back, Joe Brown at forty-six was still
amazingly competitive. Like so many of my generation, I had lived in
an awe of the reputation of Joe and Don Whillans that bordered on the
paranoid. It is hard now to recapture the degree to which most
climbers felt so comprehensively overwhelmed by the legendary
Rock and Ice members. Brown/Whillans routes in the Llanberis Pass
and on Clogwyn Du'r Arddu, even today, have an aura for me that is
not easily dispelled. When I first met Joe, through Mo, I was absurdly
shy and tongue-tied. He was, I suppose, the best-known personality I
had ever met and had been a hero figure to me for fifteen years. Joe was
friendly enough but there was a quality of slight remoteness in his
contained, practical, calm self that was not easy to penetrate. I always

felt that Joe, more than anyone, realised I was a complete fraud but was too polite to mention it. Many have seen in Joe an almost Oriental wisdom, enhanced by his slanting, hooded eyes that crinkle in vast amusement at the foibles of human nature. Very little seems to shock him and his flat, down-to-earth common-sense appraisal of others is invariably accurate and perceptive. As the trip progressed I found him more and more amusing, with a fund of stories from many past expeditions. His language was quite appalling when he was out with the boys, though in normal company Joe was the perfect gentleman. Attempting to mend a broken Primus stove at Base Camp, Joe gave up in disgust. 'The fucking fucker's fucked,' he explained succinctly. 'Fuck it,' he added as an afterthought.

Twelve years ago I wrote of Joe's uncanny ability to keep climbing at a high standard but that I imagined that Trango would be his swan-song – how wrong I was! Since then Joe has been away on innumerable trips to India, Pakistan, South America (on optimistic treasure hunts with Hamish MacInnes) and, most recently, to Tibet and Everest itself. He is now sixty, and still as competitive as ever. In the mild January of 1989 I made (by my standards) a good start to the year doing fifty rock climbs by the end of the month. 'I've only done five,' Joe said. 'But they were all new. And long. And hard. Ha, ha, ha.' Joe's laugh is one of the great sounds of British climbing. Joe has the ability to come out on top of every encounter without trying. Geoff Birtles, editor of *High* magazine, once told him that even after knowing him for twenty years he still felt that Joe exercised a kind of power over him.

Joe looked faintly puzzled. 'Why do you bother to open the door when I come and see you then, you prat?'

'You've just done it again,' Geoff replied miserably.

Malcolm Howells was the fourth climbing member of the Trango team. A mathematician with a PhD, Malcolm was the expedition doctor (he was, after all, entitled to be so addressed). His knowledge of the subject was rudimentary but Malcolm is nothing if not conscientious. Each night on the walk-in he would be surrounded by porters and villagers with all-too-real as well as many imaginary ailments. Aspirins were the normal placebo with the occasional course of antibiotics for seriously ill patients. These seemed to us to be nearly as miraculous in their effects as they were to the recipients, who often came back from death's door. Malcolm had a very British bedside manner and on one occasion was heard to advise a scantily clad porter shaking with fever, 'Wrap up warm and have an early night.' To which Mo added, 'And don't forget the electric blanket.' On two subsequent expeditions I have passed the same windswept spot and laughed at the memory of Malcolm's well-meaning suggestion.

Malcolm was more than puzzled at my emotional responses to situations and maintained a rational and calm front to everything. His classic comment on crossing the heaving, white water chaos of the Panmah River by a plaited birch twig bridge (now mercifully deceased) was, 'It's not logical to be scared.' He was mildly amused at how impressed I had been by the first view of Trango and told me that it was exactly as he had imagined it. But Malcolm did have his humorous moments and could recite ('sing' is too strong a word, for he is completely tone deaf) the Philosophers' Song from *Monty Python's Flying Circus*, with the immortal lines: 'Aristotle, Aristotle, was a bugger for the bottle . . . René Descartes was a drunken old fart, "I drink therefore I am" . . . Socrates himself is particularly missed, a lovely little thinker but a bugger when he's pissed.' Walking up the couloir to the bottom of the Tower one could occasionally hear Malcolm's slow, one-note rendering of 'Take a Pair of Sparkling Eyes', a melancholy dirge that suited the misery of the interminable scree slope that led to the Boulder at the foot of the Tower where we had our Advance Base.

Tony, despite collecting a couple of quite gigantic blisters on his heels during the walk-in that must have been horribly painful to endure day after day, was always fitter and stronger than I and this continued on the lower reaches of the Tower itself. Old fixed rope from the previous year was slowly uncovered and occasionally replaced until a camp could be established on the Snow Patch at around a third of the way up the Tower. Above that the route steepened considerably into a series of almost vertical cracks and corners up to the point where Martin had had his epic fight with his trapped knee. Though we shared the filming it was quite clear that there was no room for both of us all the way up the climb and that Tony was coping far better than I with both the steep jumaring and the stress of filming. There was not much point in bemoaning my fate, and after one visit to the Snow Patch Camp, which I found utterly exhausting, I realised that, barring misfortunes or miracles (depending which way you looked at it), that was about as far as I was likely to get. I was disappointed, but not excessively so, for the weeks of effort to get there had been immensely rewarding and I know that I had no real pretension to be a hero. I had found out that it takes quite a lot of strength and courage simply to exist on a mountain like Trango and that I didn't have enough. It was really as simple as that.

The others slowly regained the highpoint of 1975 until just below

Martin's infamous crack when a violent storm sent all of us off back to Base Camp for a few days' rest. Time was slipping away and our porters were due to return after only three weeks. Obviously this would not be long enough and I retreated to Paiju to try and get a message to them to wait there with supplies of wood and shelter until we had finished the climb. On my return to Base Camp the others set off for what we knew would be the final attempt.

I decided to go back up to Advance Base and visit the snowy col separating the Tower from one of its smaller satellite peaks. I could also film the action high on the Tower through a big lens, though I had no illusions that this would contribute more than a very minor part to the film. What I thought would be an uneventful little foray turned out to be my closest ever brush with death.

It was a glorious day and during my pauses for cigarettes and drinks from the melt-water trickling down the couloir, I felt surprisingly content to be on my own in the superb setting. Because it was so hot I was following the gully bed where it was cooler. I reached the last resting place, a slight flattening above some prominent boulders and below the final rise to the tent. I noticed the avalanche snow was fast disappearing, and that Trango was as free from snow as I had seen it. Sitting on the scree I had a final smoke before the last slog up to the Boulder.

As I finished my cigarette I heard a grinding, bumping sound above the noise of the stream. Turning round and looking up, I saw a large boulder bouncing slowly down the gully bed. Harmless enough; I was wondering where it had come from. The obvious danger was in random stones falling from the side walls of the gully, and this one hadn't come from there. Looking up again I saw a sight that I will never forget. A few hundred feet above, the couloir was full of huge boulders, bouncing and crashing down towards me. I could see boulders tossed into the air and breaking up and by now could hear the horrifying rattle and roar as they approached.

It is a cliché to say that time stood still, or that my heart missed a beat, but something very like that happened. I stood transfixed, gaping at what seemed to be the last sight I would ever see before being plucked away down the couloir to be smashed into many pieces. There was no shelter to aim for, and no point in looking, for the boulders were already upon me. Thumping and whirring down the gully, the first salvo shot past on either side. As they did so I had time to realise that my position, given the circumstances, wasn't so bad as it could have been. I was standing on the middle of a division of the stream bed. Some way above was another boulder which, though giving no obvious protection, was diverting the rocks down the little gullies on either side. Praying that this would continue, the second and major wave of boulders came grinding down accompanied by a mass of muddy water.

I had picked up my sack and was holding it in front of me, a feeble gesture if a big one scored a direct hit. Some of the larger boulders were the size of pianos. I was beginning to think I was leading a charmed life, when a real monster exploded on the rock above me: one half went whipping into the gully bed on my left, bounced out and came spinning towards me. Holding my sack I dodged – the sack was removed from my hands with the ease of a conjuring trick, and I was left to evade the remnants of the other half.

The rocks were not travelling very fast. At times huge piles would almost stop, before gathering momentum and rolling inexorably on. I had time to see it all happening. After a third smaller wave of stones had bounded past and out of sight, it began to occur to me that I had got away with it. On either side was a brown foaming torrent of muddy water and the gullies were scoured deep by the passage of the rock fall. It was clear what had caused it. The rocks had descended from the right-hand side of the Tower, out of the hideous-looking gully between it and Trango Peak. The sudden increase in temperature must have caused a huge build-up of melt-water to accumulate, before upsetting the balance and causing the whole scree slope to lose its stability.

I found I was shaking violently. After a few moments, certain that there was no more to come, I risked a look round for my sack. It contained a sleeping-bag, duvet, two cameras and various lenses. I assumed I had lost the lot, and was amazed, looking down the couloir, to pick it out, about a hundred metres lower, jammed in a wide crack high out of the gully bed. I summoned up the courage to scramble down and retrieve it, covered in mud but still intact as, unbelievably, were its contents.

By comparison my solo excursion to the col the next day was a delight, cramponing up crisp, hard névé and gaining height fast. The view from the knife-edge of snow at the top was stunning: the Baltoro Cathedrals, great gothic triangles of orange granite, the Mustagh Tower and an unusual view of Gasherbrum I, or Hidden Peak. To my right the colossal North-East Face of Trango Tower seemed utterly blank and featureless for almost all its 1000 metres.

Back at Advance Base I could see tiny figures high on the route and a figure, which I assumed was Martin, ascending the Boysen Crack, as it was now called. Later in the afternoon all four climbers, plus Tony, disappeared from view and I returned, this time very warily, down the couloir to Base Camp.

As luck would have it it was Martin who got the chance to do battle with 'his' crack and, as he said later, 'It was with some pounding of the old heart that I regained my highpoint and smashed a large bong [piton] into the exact spot I had jammed my knee.' Above that Martin found that the climbing was still desperate and progress could once more only be made by knee jamming! At last the angle eased off and he gained the security of some snowy ledges that would make a reasonable bivouac site.

The summit chimneys so obvious from below turned out to be huge blank corners seamed with ice. Mo's 'three pitches' were wildly optimistic and two more days' extremely hard climbing were needed before a snowy Shoulder was reached, some hundred metres below the top of the Tower. Far below at Base Camp I scanned the Upper Tower with a large mirror lens on one of the still cameras. Suddenly, I spotted two tiny dots just below the summit. As I watched one of the figures appeared on the summit itself. Even from around three miles and 2500 metres I could tell it was Mo. The other figure was just as obviously Martin and he soon joined him. For Mo two years of planning and dogged effort had finally paid off. 'We looked around and I thought, oh, fantastic, I could stay here for ever.' Martin looked in wonder up the Baltoro: 'Masherbrum, Gasherbrum, Mustagh Tower, K2 up in the clouds – just incredible.'

As darkness fell two very tired climbers abseiled down to the bivouac ledges. Out of food and fuel Joe and Malcolm spent a pensive night, neither wanting to go to the top but neither wanting to let the other down. The weather showed signs of breaking again, but they left at first light and quickly climbed the fixed ropes left by Martin and Mo. Tony had made it to the snow Shoulder just below the top but had been unable to complete the climb though, as Joe said, he'd done everything else but.

And so the Trango Tower was climbed. At the time it ranked with Changabang's West Face, climbed by Peter Boardman and Joe Tasker a few months later, as being one of the hardest technical rock climbs achieved in the Himalaya. For many years Trango awaited a second ascent and it was not until 1987 that a French team succeeded on a new route just to the left of ours. They also made a parapente descent of the Tower, a quite horrifying concept. I cannot imagine just how terrifying it must be, having completed over a thousand metres of vertical or overhanging climbing, to finish by throwing yourself off the top with just a flimsy rectangle of nylon between you and eternity!

Mo, exuberant the day after climbing Trango Tower.

Looking back thirteen years, a lot seems to have changed in the world of expedition climbing. On Trango we had no Gore-tex clothing or tents and no plastic boots. Mo was the only one of us to wear salopettes and though we all wore fabric-pile jackets they were still quite primitive designs. A lot of our fixed rope was heavy, we had no Friends (camming devices) and relied on heavy pegs and bongs. Our route was clearly achieved siege-style, though we had no porter support and in reality were a four-man team. It has since been a source of mild irritation that many similar expeditions have described their ascents as alpine-style or lightweight without significantly differing from our own tactics. Similarly, any technical climbing has tended to be reported as 'the hardest ever undertaken at altitude', but until very recent developments (some of which have been on the Trango Towers themselves) it would be fair to say that little if anything matched the sustained technical difficulty of the original route on the Tower. More seriously, recent events on bigger peaks seem to show a scant regard for safety and appalling risks have been undertaken for the dubious satisfaction of a 'first'. Corners have been cut, regulations broken and lives put at unnecessary risk. But these are subjects best dealt with elsewhere and should not be allowed to blur the memory of what Mo described as 'that immaculate pile of rock, the best climbing that any of us had ever experienced'.

The expedition taught Tony and me invaluable lessons, about care and maintenance of equipment, about the problems of handling movie film in extreme conditions and of the sheer difficulty of getting good footage at high altitude. In the end the film, which I suppose goes under the heading of a heroic failure, is still, with all its imperfections, a moving little testimony to the spirit of the expedition. It also marked the beginning of a long and fruitful association with Chameleon Films in Leeds. Allen Jewhurst and Chris Lister were just forming an independent film company and this was one of their first ventures. Through thick and thin we have battled on over the years, not without some severe disagreements over editorial decisions. Despite this, I am still very proud of all the films I have made with Chris and Allen.

Ever since the July day in 1976 when I turned my back on the great granite obelisk and started the walk home I have been irredeemably hooked on the Himalaya: the place, the people, the mountains and the climbing. Trango was the catalyst for a decade of obsessive travel, films and adventure that seems to lead inexorably back to the Karakoram in 1986, to K2 and disaster.

6

BARNAJ II, CLIMBERS NIL

THOUGH THE overland drive to India, with its echoes of flower power, spiritual discovery and drugs is now a fading memory for the middle-aged, it was still, in 1976–7, something of an adventure. I am pleased to have done the journey twice, if only to remind myself what a long way it is. These days expeditions merely sit on a 747 for a few hours and there is no sense of achievement in getting there. Not, of course, that the drive is a big deal – there are good roads all the way and, as Mo said before setting off for Trango, if the van makes it over the Llanberis Pass it should be all right for the rest of the journey.

In 1976 I had returned overland from Trango with Mo, Martin and Tony in the said van. The following year I was going a bit further east to Kashmir and a little-known mountain called Barnaj II. This expedition was the brainchild of Geoff Tier, a climber from Reading, whose company I was to share on several adventures. Geoff had invited Paul Nunn and Bob Toogood to strengthen his comparatively inexperienced team, and Paul suggested I came along to make a film for British Leyland of the overland drive in one of their new Sherpa vans. Geoff, Bob and I were to drive to Delhi to pick up the rest of the team who were flying out.

Geoff and Bob were poles apart in background and attitude: Geoff, eminently respectable middle-class, yet developing all the signs of a genuine eccentric British explorer; Bob, a tool-maker from Sheffield, was a vastly experienced climber and caver in Scotland, the Alps and in some of Europe's biggest and deepest caves. With his terrierlike determination, he frequently rose to the occasion when others flagged. The three of us made a strange team.

Driving across Turkey, after an uneventful journey through

Europe, we entered the faintly surreal world of Middle-Eastern road users. At the end of a long day we were driving in deep dusk down a series of hairpin bends. Bob, at the wheel, prided himself (with good reason) on being a fast, competent driver. Suddenly on a particularly appalling bend we were overtaken by a tractor! Not just a tractor, for it was towing a trailer; not only that, but it was freewheeling with no lights on! Cut to the quick, Bob tried to retrieve his honour but to no avail. We watched in amazement tinged with horror as the crazy apparition hurtled, apparently out of control, away from us and into the night, never to be caught or seen again.

At each border Bob and I would steel ourselves as Geoff, who at the time worked as a town-planner in Slough Town Hall, tackled customs officials head on, using British adminspeak to combat the interminable machinations of Oriental officialdom. But Geoff has the unhappy knack of invariably misunderstanding what he is being told and the Iranian/Afghanistan border was the scene for one of his best ever performances. Bob and I could hardly bear to watch as he entered into the spirit of the thing. Endless forms and misunderstandings later an official was demanding to inspect a tin-opener in box seventeen, buried in the depths of the van and taking hours to unpack.

'Show him your penknife, that's got a tin-opener on it.'

'But it's not the right one,' protested Geoff.

'Just do it,' I hissed through clenched teeth as Bob beat his head against the door.

Afghanistan was even hotter than I remembered. On the dead straight roads through the deserts, with the hint of mountains on the horizon, I found a real satisfaction in the boundless space and empty blue sky. It was the taste of Central Asia and one to which, over the years, I have become more and more addicted. We entered Pakistan over the Khyber Pass and drove via Peshawar to spend a couple of days in Islamabad before the last leg to Delhi.

We arrived in the late evening at the British Embassy Club to be greeted by friends from the year before and were told the first details of a dramatic story that had been enacted near the summit of the Ogre, a hitherto unclimbed 7285-metre mountain on the Biafo Glacier. We had apparently missed seeing Nick Estcourt by half an hour. He had just left for the airport and a flight home. He was the last to depart. Doug Scott had broken both his legs, Chris Bonington his ribs and Mo and Clive Rowland had been involved in a protracted epic to get them both down in one piece.

The staff of the British Embassy in Islamabad have over the years extended a warm welcome to British climbers in Pakistan and many friendships with embassy staff have developed. On this occasion, however, I tested their tolerance to the limit. After the journey I decided to give the film gear a good clean, and charge all the batteries. I opened the back door of the van. No camera, no aluminium case. I opened the passenger door and looked under the seats. No camera. Weak at the knees, I checked again. And again. Oh my God, I'd left the bloody thing on the side of the road on the Khyber Pass.

I settled down to a day of sorrow-drowning. That evening I told my tale of woe to anyone in the bar who would listen. At one point someone overheard me. 'That's funny, someone rang the embassy to report finding a camera.'

'Who? Where? When?'

'I don't know, I just heard it sometime today.'

'Please, oh please think.'

'Ah, I remember, it came through on the switchboard – a call from Peshawar.'

'What did you do with it?'

'I wrote the number down on a piece of paper.'

'Where is it?'

'I don't know.'

'Oh, Christ, think, man, think.'

'I'll go to the embassy and have a look.'

Moaning quietly to myself, we drove the half-mile or so to the main embassy building. Inside, my possible saviour started looking aimlessly through a wastepaper-bin.

'I'll help you.'

'Oh, no you won't; it's classified.'

'But it's rubbish.'

'It's still classified.'

Half an hour later he gave up. 'It's no good, it's not here.'

I slumped on my chair in despair.

'I wonder, can I remember the name? I'll look in the Peshawar telephone directory.'

This man, I thought through clenched teeth (it is possible to think through clenched teeth), is stark, staring, totally, out to lunch, round the twist, barking mad. How can he possibly in a million, squillion years read a sodding telephone directory full of Alis, Mohammeds, Khans, Hussains and Shahs and pick the right one?

After five minutes, he looked up. 'Got it already,' he said cheerfully. 'I remember now, it was a hotel,' and he started dialling the number. After an age of crossed lines and false starts he got through. Yes, a camera had been found, a movie camera. On the Khyber Pass, yesterday. Yes, it could be collected. Tomorrow? First thing – well, eleven a.m. He put the phone down. 'So glad we could help you.' I could have kissed him.

Next morning saw me and the van racing back to Peshawar, gripped and nervous that something would even now go wrong. After many enquiries I found the hotel, a big, modern building in a secluded suburb. The manager invited me into his office. We drank tea and talked of this and that. Out of the corner of my eye I could see the precious aluminium case.

'The camera?' I enquired at last.

'Ah, yes, the camera. I am delighted it has been found and you can now take it with you. But there is just one small problem.'

'Oh, yes – of course.' (How much should I give him – one hundred, two hundred rupees?)

'No, no, no, it is not money, it is this: how can I be sure that the camera belongs to you?'

People have killed for less. Because, you utter imbecile, I thought to myself, I would hardly have rung you up and driven all the bloody way because I just happened to think you might possibly be giving away spare movie cameras to the first person who fancies one.

Total impasse.

'I can tell you what's inside the case,' I suggested.

He shook his head regretfully.

'I can tell you the exact make of camera and how much film is in it.'

Still not good enough.

'I can write the film company's name and address on a piece of paper and this will match the address inside the box.'

'So it is not actually your own camera?'

God give me strength.

Suddenly he tired of the game. 'Okay, take it. It is yours.' I nearly wept with gratitude.

After that the rest of the journey, through the Punjab via Lahore and down to Delhi, seemed something of an anticlimax. But the drive up to the mountain village of Kishtwar was a spectacular and at times frightening last lap. Frequently the van would be creeping round corners poised over colossal drops. Indian road signs like 'The Icy Finger of Death Points at the Speed King' or 'Marry Safety, Divorce Speed', were scarcely reassuring, neither were the ornate jangling lorries belching fumes and sidling crabwise along the twisting dirt road, their chassis and axles knocked out of alignment by many near-terminal encounters. Occasionally a memorial plaque with a long list of names would mark the post where a bus had gone over the edge.

At last we were gaining real height and the humidity of the plains gave way to simple heat. As we toiled slowly up one last twisting hill the view opened up to the cloud-laden Himalayan foothills. It was journey's end as far as the van was concerned and the start of some long overdue exercise for us.

Kishtwar (in the state of Jammu and Kashmir) is set in the foothills of the Indian Himalaya above the great River Chenab. It is a small and quite attractive town, with a huge *maidan* or village green sweeping away from the old-fashioned Dak bungalow, a cheap rest-house for travellers, in which we were staying. Outside the bungalow came the noise I will always associate with Barnaj – the sound of mules and donkeys braying. They were being loaded for the fifty-mile journey up to Machail, the last village before our Base Camp.

About two weeks had passed since we had arrived in Delhi and suffered the normal birth pangs of an Indian mountaineering expedition. No Liaison Officer was ready for us and until we had one we couldn't attempt to climb the mountain. Eventually, to keep moving and save money, Paul, Geoff Smith and I decided to walk in with the mules, leaving Geoff Tier and the others to wait for the arrival of the LO.

The first night was spent in the village of Shasoo in a cave under a huge rock, strangely reminiscent of the Chiddingly Wood cave years before. Up at dawn for a quick brew of tea and a few biscuits, then off into the cool of the morning, at first wearing a polar jacket and walking fast to keep warm, then, as the sun rose, it was down to T-shirt and shorts and the usual trekking game of hunt-the-shade. Even patches of sunlight in the woods were uncomfortably hot, but on the third day, as we gained height up the banks of the Bhut River, it became more bearable with the odd breath of cool mountain breeze drying the sweat on our brows. It was on this last leg that I set up a complex film shot that was intended to be rather clever.

Above a wooden bridge was a densely vegetated bank of wild cannabis through which the path wound its way. Looking back I could just see the bridge through the leaves. I decided to wait for the mules to cross and start the shot with the cannabis leaves in close-up focus. Then, as the mules reached the middle of the bridge I would pull focus to the mules and zoom out to show the whole scene. I set up camera and tripod and practised the shot. Inevitably three or four children materialised out of the depths of the woods. They watched, as all Indian children do, in silent, open-mouthed wonder as I waited. At last I heard the tinkling sound of the bells around the mules' necks that warned of their approach. Concentrating, I started the shot.

Suddenly all the foliage disappeared from the frame. What the . . . ?
Opening my non-viewfinder eye I saw what had happened. The little
buggers! Trying to help and unable to understand my desire for an
artistic foreground, the kids had pulled all the branches out of the way
to give me an unimpeded view. It was as severe a form of film
criticism as I had come across: worse than Allen at Chameleon
winding some of my best shots from Trango straight into the bin.
This time the shot had been edited out before it was even finished!
Serves me right for being pretentious, I thought as I packed up and set
off to catch up the others.

Machail is a small Hindu village with its own tiny temple. We
arrived and checked into the police post where a young policeman,
stupefied with boredom at having to live in such a remote outpost,
welcomed our arrival as a heaven-sent relief from monotony. In my
limited experience of police forces around the world, his delight was
only to be matched by that of a Peruvian policeman I met in similar
isolated circumstances some years later.

Our friendly cop allowed us to camp in his back garden. Paul and
Geoff Smith wanted to press on the next day to explore alternative
approaches to the mountain. This left me with no choice but to spend a
few days on my own in Machail looking after the gear until the others
arrived. I was more than happy to do this. It was a nice place and, at
just under 3000 metres, meant I could do some very minimal acclimatising simply by sitting around doing nothing. A couple of days passed
uneventfully, then things started to happen. The first was a Hindu
festival to mark the birthday of the god Shiva. A colourful procession
of beautiful sari-clad young women, and rather grubby menfolk,
playing a variety of musical instruments with no obvious skill, beat,
clapped and blew their way with joyful abandon to the temple. It was a
heaven-sent opportunity to film and the villagers seemed delighted
that I did so.

The second event was the arrival of a visiting schools inspector who
invited me to his lodgings for afternoon tea. At least that's what I
thought I was going to. The reality was that I got hopelessly, roaring
drunk with an immensely stout and dignified old Indian gentleman
who had graduated from Oxford University before the war. He was a
fascinating man with a wonderful turn of phrase – 'This gentleman has
a delightful style of laughter', was how he introduced me to a visitor
who arrived in mid-afternoon to bring a gift of another bottle of rice
wine.

Early evening came and I was barely able to stand up. Full of booze,
chappatis, goat's cheese and eggs, I weaved an unsteady course back to

the police station and all the gear which I had cheerfully abandoned for the last few hours. I arrived to find Geoff Tier, John Escott, Rick Walters and our Liaison Officer, Captain Amarjeet Singh, in residence. They seemed somewhat grumpy and Geoff explained that they had arrived in the afternoon and set about making a meal. They had boiled potatoes in a pressure cooker, potatoes that I had bartered successfully for earlier in the day in exchange for two packets of digestive biscuits. They had tasted awful and it was a few minutes before they realised that they had boiled them in paraffin by mistake. How they had avoided blowing themselves up and taking most of Machail with them as they released the pressure on the cooker was a mystery. But they seemed more concerned that they were still hungry. I'm afraid I was unsympathetic and retired, chuckling insanely to myself, to bed and a subsequent headache.

Paul and Geoff Smith returned on the following day. They had been to the Hagshu Pass, which crosses the main Himalayan watershed into Ladakh, and seen our mountain from a distance, but it was clear that the best approach would be up the Barnaj Nullah from Machail. They also saw and photographed the spectacular North Face of Hagshu Peak, a mountain that has since been attempted on several occasions and was finally climbed in 1989.

It took a couple of days to organise mules and porters to get us to Base Camp, another two days on from Machail, and some 1000 metres higher. A long steep path through woods led to an idyllic flat-bottomed valley floor at the foot of the Barnaj Glacier. We bivouacked under huge boulders at a site obviously used by shepherds tending their summer flocks of sheep and goats. I was half wakened in the night by a violent rattle of hailstones. It seemed curious that they had managed to blow to the back of the cave and I snuggled deeper into my sleeping-bag. In the morning I awoke to the sight of a goat's bottom filling my field of vision and realised that they hadn't been hailstones after all.

Barnaj II is a complex rather than beautiful peak and from our limited view at Base Camp it was obvious that our initial choice of route, from a distant photograph, would be too hard and dangerous. Instead we opted for a long and devious route that would eventually lead us to the South Ridge of the mountain. The first two weeks were spent load-carrying in appalling weather to establish Camp 1. A large snow basin beyond led us, we hoped, to a point where we could get onto the upper section of the ridge. Illness and lack of acclimatisation had taken their toll and so it was down to Paul and the two Geoffs and me to make a realistic assault on the mountain, if and when the weather let up. My role as film-maker meant that I could do little except try and keep up with Geoff Tier, with whom I was climbing most of the time. The longer I spent with Geoff the better I got on with him for, despite our very different attitudes to life and the occasional irritation we had caused each other on the drive, we had remained friends and have done so to this day.

Endless floundering through waist-deep powder snow got us to the foot of a long couloir leading to an obvious shelf below the South Peak of Barnaj II. The couloir was straightforward but potentially dangerous. Paul had fixed rope up most of its 250-metre length, anchoring it to the side walls with good rock anchors. Whether or not the ropes would hold in the event of the gully avalanching was a moot point. As it didn't we never found out. But, as with so much Himalayan climbing, it was best not to have too vivid an imagination as slow progress was made kicking into the bottomless powder and hauling unashamedly on the rope.

Unlike the obvious charms of rock climbing, snow-flogging at altitude is not a pleasant activity. It is dull, repetitive and possibly hazardous. Yet the first time I climbed the gully was as near a justification for Himalayan climbing as I can ever give. We had set out with the idea of going lightweight up the gully, pitching two tunnel tents at the end of the shelf and then going for the top.

On a dreary day of thick cloud I jumared last up the fixed ropes, with quite a heavy sack of personal, film and camera gear. Above, the snowy shelf seemed to go on for ever, steepening towards the site where we hoped to pitch the two tents. I felt weary and dispirited as in early twilight, I started up the last hundred-metre slope. Then gradually, magically, the world was transformed. Great boiling layers of cloud broke up; a stray shaft of evening sun caught the summit rocks high above us, turning them a flaming orange. Through the layers of cloud the distant Brammah peaks thrust their elegant summits, and mountain after mountain emerged from the cloud, which seemed to be sinking to the valley bottoms. It was a heart-stopping moment. Even at the time I could see that the light and the weather were very reminiscent of Doug Scott's summit photographs on Everest in 1975. Despite our lowly altitude (a mere 5500 metres) I felt ridiculously happy and fulfilled just to be there. The aches went out of my legs and my breathing returned to somewhere near normal. The clouds drifted past and the light changed every few seconds. Then suddenly it all finished. The sun went below the horizon, the temperature plummeted and after a few minutes of flat calm, a bitter breeze got up. Paul and the two Geoffs had almost finished cutting the platforms for the

tunnel tents. Once they were pitched, we were inside unpacking
sleeping-bags and trying not to get snow over everything. Within an
hour we were warm and brewing up the first of several cups of sweet
tea. I was at peace with the world. The last hour had justified for me
the whole expedition; all the effort was worth it, just to enjoy those
few moments of consummate well-being.

The similarity to Doug's photos was maintained the next day with
the arrival of a violent storm, just as had happened in 1975 when Mick
Burke disappeared near the summit of Everest. We managed one
more day's climbing before being forced to retreat to the same site as
the previous night. We were reluctant to descend and spent four more
nights in tents threatened by avalanche-prone slopes. I was learning
the hard way that, unlike Trango, many expeditions fail through no
fault of their own. When the storm cleared briefly it was obvious that
an army of climbers would make little progress on the upper part of
the ridge and, reluctantly, for he had planned and led the expedition
with constant commitment and enthusiasm, Geoff Tier decided to
abandon the attempt.

What might be seen as a bit of a non-event I can now see taught me
valuable lessons, both in survival and in coming to terms with what
the mountains have to offer. Success is not always simply measured in
reaching the summit. Even the walk-out, not normally described in
expedition literature, was an experience that still sticks in my mind,
not least because of an epic thirty-five-mile stage on the very last day
back to Kishtwar with frost-numbed and badly bruised feet.

One minor success was our little film, produced for British Leyland
and subsequently used by them at the Motor Show and their own
conferences. It was a slick, snappy production and very different to
every other film I have made. It certainly gave us the enthusiasm to
carry on, for my confidence had been badly shaken with the technical
inadequacies of the Trango film. How I regretted that I had not had
the Barnaj experience before Trango. My desire to make the best
Himalayan climbing film of all time was still unfulfilled. Though the
spark still burned bright, it was to be another four years before I would
have the chance to try again. Two more expeditions in 1978 and 1979
were both unsuccessful and produced no film at all, though both in
their own ways were well worth going on. The first was to Choktoi, a
shapely granite peak on the Choktoi Glacier in the Karakoram with
Dave Potts, Malcolm Howells and Barry Whybrow. It was a trip that
Mo labelled the British Rhododendron-Crushers Expedition, main-
taining that the summit was actually lower than Base Camp. In fact
the mountain was too hard and the weather was too bad. Though only

a minor peak, it is still unclimbed and would be a worthy objective for a small expedition.

The second was a return to Barnaj, this time just four of us, Paul Nunn, John Yates, Tony Riley and me. Paul and John made a very good attempt and reached the South Peak before an impending storm forced a retreat from the summit ridge. Tony and I also had a go and were stopped in almost exactly the same place as we had been two years earlier in an identical storm. I was mildly amused to retrieve a small bundle of wire nuts clipped to a peg at our highpoint. They were actually my own, abandoned in 1977. It seemed a very expensive way to reclaim them.

7

FILMING THE BAT

BY 1979 I had made three films, *A Great Effort*, *Trango* and *Barnaj*, and failed on a fourth, for our Choktoi expedition had been such a non-event that Chameleon Films had not even bothered to process the film. The trouble with expeditions, I was fast realising, is that what actually happens is largely out of a film-maker's control. Many, if not most, Himalayan expeditions fail and it needs a clairvoyant to pick the one that will make a good film. I found myself thinking of a follow-up to *A Great Effort*, a film that recreated a real event and one that would already have the ingredients of a good story. Several alpine projects were obvious: the Eiger was rich in epics, the Frêney Pillar disaster perhaps, or the Matterhorn. But all were rather too well known and filming in the Alps seemed to be trespassing on continental film-maker's territory (as well as being very expensive). I racked my brains for an idea I could get enthused over and suddenly remembered a possibility that I had discarded four years previously.

One of the great classic articles in post-war British climbing was written by Robin Smith and called 'The Bat and the Wicked'. It describes in compelling prose the first attempts and eventual ascent of the Bat, a rock climb on Ben Nevis that in 1959 was one of the hardest routes in Scotland. Smith, one of Scotland's leading lights of the late 'fifties, was also a brilliant writer. He had made the ascent in the company of the young Dougal Haston with whom he had been compelled to join forces. Haston had also written about the climb in his autobiography, *In High Places*, which gave a rather different perspective. It had seemed an obvious and brilliant subject for a film but in 1975 there were two almost insurmountable problems: Robin Smith had been killed with Wilfrid Noyce in the Pamirs in 1962. Haston was still very much alive, and a major figure in the mountaineering world, but I couldn't imagine him being interested in playing himself as a youth, and found it equally hard to envisage anyone else capable of acting the part, so the idea languished. But since

I had first considered it, Haston himself had been killed in a skiing accident near his home in Leysin in early 1977. Now, two years later, it seemed perfectly acceptable to re-enact the story and the film could be a minor memorial to two of Scotland's greatest mountaineers.

First things first. Tony Riley and I had gone our separate ways in the last two years and it was now time to work together again. I applied to the Yorkshire Arts Association in Bradford for financial backing and received a small but invaluable grant that would just cover the actual cost of filmstock, processing, camera hire etc. Paul Nunn was quickly roped in as safety officer and general climbing supervisor. The only problem was the two main 'actors'. They had to be climbers first and foremost, able to perform in front of the camera and if possible bear a vague resemblance to the characters, though this was asking a lot. However, they didn't need to be Scottish, as the bulk of the film would be narrated and what little dialogue there was could be dubbed in later on. Alan Rouse, whom I had got to know reasonably well in the last two years, was keen to act the part of Dougal Haston, but in the end found himself committed to guiding in Peru during the period we needed him. Brian Hall took his place. He had climbed extensively with Al in South America and, with Rab Carrington, Roger Baxter-Jones and Al, had just made an extremely bold alpine-style ascent of Jannu in Nepal. Brian was calm, capable and utterly reliable. He would be ideal, as would Rab Carrington who, after some initial misgivings, agreed to play the part of Robin Smith.

The two things that worried Brian and Rab were that they both had to fall off in front of the cameras from a point halfway up the great Carn Dearg Buttress on Ben Nevis, and also that they would have to have short haircuts. In Rab's case this would also mean the removal of his piratical black beard, of which he was very proud. But Rab eventually agreed to subjugate himself for the sake of art.

Two days later Rab and Al Rouse went soloing on an unfrequented buttress on Froggatt Edge. Rab had got himself irreversibly committed just below the top of the crag, about fifteen metres above a boulder-strewn landing. Al had rushed round to the top to try and help and had stuck his foot over the edge for Rab to grab. But Rab, his strength ebbing, couldn't let go with either hand. Al said that he was actually biting at tufts of grass in his last efforts to stay in contact with the rock. Then with a yell he was off. Al ran back down to the bottom, fearing the worst, and was amazed to find Rab had managed to land between the projecting rocks and was still very much alive. Al ran down to the Chequers pub on Froggatt Hill to telephone for an ambulance. As he entered the bar the landlord asked what he wanted.

'A pint of bitter,' said Al automatically, before remembering why he was there.

I went to visit Rab in the Hallamshire Hospital in Sheffield to cheer him up and see if he was still on for the summer shoot. 'I know you wanted the starring role, Rab, but I didn't expect you to take the audition quite so seriously.'

Thankfully, Rab had got off very lightly with a dislocated elbow and chipped bone in his knee. He seemed confident that he would be okay in time, though now the thought of deliberately falling off must have been even less attractive.

The weekend before we were due to drive up to Scotland my girlfriend Laraine and I went as usual to the Moon on Saturday evening. The pub was crowded and it was a warm night. Doug Scott and a team of Nottingham climbers were sitting on the car park wall. 'Get inside, youth, and have a look. Robin Smith's in there!' Puzzled, I pushed my way into the bar. Rab, hair shorn and clean shaven, was completely transformed and bore an uncanny resemblance to one haunting photo I had seen of Smith looking stern and worried.

'I've just been talking to Keith Myhill,' he told me. Keith was a well-known Sheffield climber and old friend of Rab's. 'After five minutes and Keith getting more and more confused – "You know who I am, don't you?" I asked him. "Er yes, yes, of course." But it was obvious he hadn't a bloody clue!'

We drove up to Scotland, the five of us in a borrowed Volvo estate packed to the roof with film, climbing and camping equipment and food. As we drove off the M6 and on to the A74 over the Scottish border, big drops of summer rain splattered the windscreen. Not for the first time I questioned the wisdom of our venture. Filming in summer, on the Ben, and in early August, ran the risk of a total washout. We had a week at the most to do the shoot, after which we would all be going different ways. A half-finished film might remain so indefinitely. Also, despite a lot of preliminary work on the shooting script, breaking the story down into scenes, there were far more imponderables to deal with than on the making of *A Great Effort*. Only Rab and Paul had climbed on Carn Dearg Buttress before and Tony and I had to rely heavily on their experience to make even the haziest plans.

We stopped in Glencoe to visit Hamish MacInnes, an old friend of Paul and Rab, to ask for advice and also the loan of some ropes to rig the various stances on the route. The 'Old Fox' listened to our plans in silence, then told us that the weather on the Ben had been poor and that he thought the Bat would be far too wet to climb. But he took us into his workshop and rummaged around in the bottom of an old trunk, before rising in triumph, clutching an ancient pair of rotting PAs (the original rock boot manufactured by Pierre Allain in France).

'These were one of my first ever pairs. I loaned them to Robin when he did the Bat – at least some of your gear will be authentic.'

We drove the remaining miles to Fort William encouraged by our visit. Not so encouraging was the knowledge that we would have to camp outside the CIC hut at the foot of Carn Dearg. The Scottish Mountaineering Club had refused to let us use the hut for the week, claiming that to do so for filming purposes would cause 'gross inconvenience to the hut-users'. As the hut was locked and empty for five out of the six nights we were there we could only assume that the 'gross inconvenience' would have been to ourselves. It seemed particularly unfair as we were trying to make a film that paid homage to two of the SMC's most illustrious members, but there was nothing to be done except to set about carting everything up the Allt a'Mhuilinn, the narrow valley below the northern cliffs of Ben Nevis and camp. Rab eyed the huge pile with distaste. 'There's more kit here than we took to Jannu last year.'

In winter I had always found the walk up to the CIC hut gruelling almost beyond human endurance. It was worse in summer: hot and humid with bottomless bogs to fall into; clouds of midges and showers of rain. We did two huge carries from the parking spot we had managed to use via the Forestry Commission tracks, which saved an hour or so. As we finished our first evening meal we could at least reflect that from now on we were at the mercy of the weather and worrying couldn't do any good at all.

Despite rain in the night it seemed a reasonable morning and we set about carrying cameras, tripod and climbing gear to the bottom of the route. The Bat, which is still graded a respectable E2, weaves a complex line. It starts up the wall to the left of the great corner of Centurion, the classic route put up by Don Whillans in the mid-1950s. The Bat crosses it after the first pitch by a delicate traverse over bottomless slabs, and then finds its way up a short overhanging groove – the Hoodie Groove, so called by Smith because 'it looked as happy as a hoodie crow'. This led to the foot of the great corner, perched high on the crag, on which most of the action would take place. Each day's filming would be more demanding than the one before with further to climb to get started. But on day one it was comparatively easy to film Brian and Rab sitting at the foot of the route, gearing up and climbing the first pitch. The corner of Centurion was repulsively wet but the walls and slabs of the Bat seemed quite dry. Higher up the Corner looked appalling but that was at least two days away.

From the start we gelled as a team. Brian and Rab showed little of the self-consciousness in front of the camera that I had found a problem on other films, and Tony and I resumed our normal working relationship. Paul encouraged and cajoled us up to stances and put in hours of work making sure each was completely bombproof. His early years of artificial climbing on Derbyshire and Yorkshire lime-stone paid off, for climbing cameramen have to be able to relax to concentrate on the job in hand. If they are worried about safety it makes a difficult job almost impossible. Jumaring and abseiling are activities that rely totally on reliable anchors. Any mishap on fixed ropes is likely to be both the first and last, so there is little scope for learning from your mistakes!

Everything on the first day ran smoothly. Rab, dressed in an old sweater and patched breeches, led the first two pitches, finishing out on the skyline on the edge of the undercut slabs, just below the Hoodie Groove. It made good filming as he traversed away from the camera with the drop below revealed with every move he made. Then Brian joined him and as he completed the pitch, the old hawser laid nylon ropes that Rab had taken in dangled free in space. They rigged an abseil that would take them straight to the ground, and also be the line of the fixed ropes for us to climb straight to the stance next day. The abseil, made against the background of stormy skies and muted colours of the Allt a'Mhuilinn, was very atmospheric. That evening we were treated to a lurid sunset through breaking clouds. Quickly I persuaded Rab and Brian to 'walk off into the sunset'. It may have been a cliché but it would be a superb finishing shot for the film.

I was apprehensive about the next day's work. Tony and I had decided to take it in turns to film on the climb itself or with the big Arriflex camera and tripod on the ground. I was going first which meant a free fifty-metre jumar up the fixed rope that had been left in place hanging over the huge roof of Sassenach, the great Brown/ Whillans climb. After Brian and Rab had reclimbed the rope they had found it already beginning to fray on the lip of the overhang, so we used another long rope as a gigantic top rope, running through an independent belay at the top and taken in at the bottom as the person ascending gained height on the fixed rope. The problem was that once off the ground, violent spinning occurred, wrapping the fixed rope round the top rope. Progress was slow and best made with the eyes firmly shut. The fragmentary views of adjacent rock and distant hillside whirling past were too horrible to watch and made me feel quite sick. I arrived with relief at the stance and soon Paul joined me and set about rigging a safe vantage-point immediately below the Hoodie Groove. Despite his best efforts, the stance was so restricted that I had great difficulty in framing the action. In the end I had to use Paul himself to steady me as I tended to pendulum slowly round on the belay pegs and end up filming empty space.

The groove was the first scene that demanded we stick exactly to the script. Haston had led this and been unable to climb it free. He had managed to flick a line sling on to a small spike away on the left wall, stand in the sling and reach for better holds above. Nowadays it is climbed free and the manoeuvre is unnecessary. I was worried that it would prove time-consuming or even impossible to get the sling on the spike (a similar, though much harder, lassoing job occurs on White Slab on Clogwyn Du'r Arddu which has been known to defeat some aspirant cowboys). So I was relieved when Brian managed it after only three or four attempts and the prospect of sending home for more film receded. Brian stood in the sling, and then made a dynamic move for the holds above, commenting with feeling that it was harder to get out of the sling than into it. He climbed quickly to the stance at the foot of the corner and soon Rab was ready to follow. I tried to vary the shots as much as possible, filming big close-ups of Rab's feet and hands on the holds in order to keep the action varied. To my delight Rab acted the 'foot in the sling' scene perfectly, for Smith had described it as 'a strange can-can move'. It was exactly that and, whether acting or not, Rab looked extremely precarious before he too lunged for the finishing holds. He joined Brian and they both spent some time eyeing up the Great Corner before descending.

It had taken all day to shoot what was eventually to be only a couple of minutes' finished film. I abseiled half fearfully, then with exhilaration out into space, spinning wildly, as on the way up, and landed about five metres away from the bottom of the crag. Tony said he had got some good long shots, which was a relief, as I had feared that I was so close to the action that it would be hard for him to film without me getting in the way.

When Rab and Brian descended the euphoria I felt about the day's work was dispelled. The Great Corner, they explained, was still damp and greasy, growing some sort of brown fungus and looking almost unclimbable. They suggested a change of plan. Tomorrow they would go up on their own and rig the whole pitch by fair means or foul. They would have hidden protection in the crack so that they could concentrate on climbing quickly in front of the cameras the following day. The plan did make sense, for it was also necessary to get some long zooms into and out of the crag with only Rab and Brian on it. Tony and I could film from the ground and also spend the day filming cutaways, shots that could be used to break up the action and help out with disparate shots that would not naturally cut together. Paul could go down to Fort William and get more food, for we had just about finished my estimated week's supply in three nights.

The weather meanwhile stayed uncannily consistent. Though it appeared to be raining everywhere else in Scotland, it stayed dry in the Allt a'Mhuilinn. Each day clouds of rain swept along the Great Glen and the summit of the Ben was normally hidden. It made for a great atmosphere and, more important, the quality of light stayed the same for the whole week which meant that there would be continuity in editing and also that shots from different days could easily be intercut. Just occasionally, it seemed, the god of film-making was prepared to give his disciples an even break.

Brian and Rab (who we now referred to as 'Dougal' and 'Robin', and who also answered to their new names) set out early as usual and slowly reascended to the bottom of the Corner, then took it in turns to lay siege to its lower reaches. We filmed them from below, trying to show the scale of the cliff. They reached the top of the Corner and left a fixed rope for Paul to use the next day to get a camera position looking down. Then they retreated once more. Paul returned from Fort William late in the afternoon carrying a satisfactorily bulging rucksack that also gave forth a promising clinking noise, as of one bottle against another.

That evening was filled with foreboding. Tomorrow was make or break day. Brian had the job of taking the first and biggest fall, after which Rab would have two shorter ones. It was to be Tony's big day as well for he would be filming from the bottom of the Corner. We had given a lot of thought to the filming of the falls for in Smith's original article he described them in vivid detail. The problem was to retain the description which took around fifteen seconds to narrate, while recording the falls which in reality lasted only a second or so. By filming simultaneously in slow motion and normal speed from three positions and by 'pruning' the narration down a bit I hoped that I could get words and actions to coincide. But the major problem was for Brian to psych himself up for the prospect of throwing himself into space halfway up a major Scottish cliff. Rather him than me, I thought, as I lay in my sleeping-bag worrying about the next day.

We were up soon after first light and once more toiled up the scree and boulder-strewn path to the foot of Carn Dearg. At the bottom Brian stripped off his old green anorak and jeans and put on a full body harness underneath, before replacing his top clothing. This was because in 1959 harnesses were not in common use and with the rope just tied round the waist in the traditional way, Brian risked internal injury. Now it looked authentic but the shock would be spread to his chest, shoulders and legs. As he jumared up the fixed ropes I muttered to Tony, 'Would you throw yourself off up there just for a hundred pounds?' (Which was all we could afford to pay our two stars.) 'I don't think I would do it for anything.'

The day seemed to last a lifetime. Slowly, meticulously, Tony, in close-up, and I from a distance, filmed Rab first and then Brian as they both 'attempted' to climb the Corner. The time drew nearer for Brian's moment of truth. In Robin Smith's account Haston, in extremis on the crux, 'threw his foot away at a straw on the right wall, then his fingers went to butter. It began under control as the bit of news "I'm off" but it must have been caught in the wind for it grew like a wailing siren to a bloodcurdling scream as a black and batlike shape came hurtling over the roof with legs splayed like webbed wings and hands hooked like a vampire's . . . I could have sworn that his teeth were fangs and his eyes were big red orbs . . .' In order to get a respectable-length fall under reasonably safe conditions Brian had placed a solid runner in the crack next to where he would come off. He then pulled up some slack from Rab at the bottom who also payed some out. In theory his fall would be controlled and stop without a huge jerk. In practice I could see from the bottom that Rab had payed out a lot of rope and I wondered if Brian realised how far he was about to plummet. All set up now, cameras focused, light meters checked again – I'm really gripped – what must Brian feel like? 'Action!' High above Brian scrabbled and clutched – then he was off – hurtling straight down, free of the rock and with great presence of mind flamboyantly somersaulting on the stretch of the rope at the bottom. 'Christ, that was impressive!' Shouted cries of relief all round as we realised he'd done at least a fifteen-metre fall, almost into Tony's camera. Great, great, great.

Then it was Rab's turn. His first fall was to be caused by standing in a sling attached to a wooden wedge which popped out of the crack. The second was when Smith, by now resorting to any means to get up the crack, pulls up on a piton and 'it leaped out with a squeak of delight, giving me no time to squeal at all before I found myself swinging about under the miserable roof again.' There was a danger that these falls coming so soon would be an anticlimax after Brian's monster flier and once again we did all we could to vary the angles as Rab did his two scarcely less impressive plummets. Then, drama over, Tony filmed Rab's progress to the top of the crack. Finally, it was time for an idea we had hatched earlier. We had an 'autoload' – a clockwork camera that took cassettes of 16 mm film and was little more than a small tin box with a lens attached. Padded with strips of Karrimat, foam and cameratape, and tied to a rope, it was set running and thrown down the Corner to give a horrifying climber's-eye-view of the fall. Tony also did the big abseil down the buttress with the autoload running, and both these shots were invaluable later on. In particular the fall shot gave just the freedom I was looking for in editing to 'stretch' the scene to match the narration.

The day was almost over. Brian descended first and quietly re-treated to his tent and into his sleeping-bag. He looked pale and we suddenly realised that he was suffering slightly from shock, which was hardly surprising. The rest of us were euphoric and knew that one more day would see us through if we worked flat out. In fact if we were lucky we could probably pack up and go down to Fort William tomorrow night. The clinking bottles were broached that evening.

Our luck continued in the morning with the early arrival of some hut-users who happily allowed us to film a scene set in the CIC hut of Smith and Haston arriving in the night, and another one of them standing dishevelled, looking evil at the doorway of the hut, glaring at 'a mighty file of pilgrims making for Ben Nevis'. Even a bunch of walkers turned up on cue for the shot. Then, while Paul and Tony did the first carry of equipment back to the car, Rab, Brian and I filmed big close-up shots of hands on holds, pitons being driven into cracks, etc, on rocks at the foot of the crag.

At last it was all in the can. I heaved a colossal sigh of relief. Tottering under the weight of our rucksacks we staggered down through the bogs and back to civilisation. But almost immediately I developed a pounding, surging headache and by the time we reached Fort William I was in the throes of a full-blooded migraine, which I hadn't suffered from since I was a teenager. With blurred vision and feeling like death warmed up I was horribly sick and then lay for hours shivering in a sleeping-bag while the others went out to celebrate properly.

Next day we set off for Sheffield in torrential rain sweeping the whole of Scotland. The cloud base was well below Carn Dearg and sheets of rain drifted across the Allt a'Mhuilinn. We couldn't stop laughing.

A week later Paul, Tony and I were to fly out to Delhi on the second Barnaj expedition. Before we went we had time to view the processed rushes of the film. They were perfect, except for some telephoto shots with a big lens that were all slightly soft. Never mind – there was more than enough material to edit. One final task remained which was to shoot a pub scene, not in Fort William but, inevitably, in the Moon. We immortalised Dennis the landlord serving Rab and Brian, then enlisted the help of Sue, Rab's wife, and Laraine to act the part of two Scots lassies. I have to say that this scene has never convinced me. The girls look far too sophisticated to have been in a pub in Fort William in 1959.

When we returned in late September, defeated yet again by Barnaj, I consoled myself with the thought that editing *The Bat* would be a lot of fun. In fact it took a year of painstaking work (admittedly intermittent and part-time) before I was satisfied with it. Most was done surreptitiously within the Faculty of Art and Design in Bristol and I became used to getting into college at six thirty in the morning for three hours before the students arrived. Like *A Great Effort*, I revelled in the gradual addition of layer upon layer of sound tracks. In particular the contrast between the two narrations, both read immaculately by Scottish actors, was a challenge in juxtaposition to achieve maximum contrast without actually destroying the continuity of the story. I was eventually very proud of the fall sequences and still, when *The Bat* is projected on a big screen, watch the audience's reaction as they physically recoil at their impact.

The film was premiered (under trying circumstances) at the first of the three Kendal Mountaineering Film Festivals that I was to become increasingly involved with. The first in February 1981 was more than a little chaotic but to my delight the film had a wonderful reception from a packed house. I was well satisfied and in the ensuing celebrations at the Brewery Arts Centre shortened my life through alcoholic poisoning by, I imagine, several months.

Though *The Bat* never made us rich, its premier at Kendal certainly led to the most wonderful opportunity for me later the same year.

8

AN INVITATION TO CHINA

I N THE autumn of 1980 my mother, who had lived for over twenty-five years after contracting breast cancer, fell ill again and in January 1981 she died peacefully. Just before her death she asked me if I was going anywhere interesting in the summer. I told her that there might be a slight chance of going to China with Chris Bonington. 'You be careful – we may meet again, sooner than you think!' It was a typical no-nonsense comment from her, reminiscent of Don Whillans in its wry and realistic judgment. Her death, while not a shock, was still a blow to me as I realised with both parents gone just how much I had relied on them. Now of course I was next in line for eternity, or oblivion – not a happy thought. My second marriage, to Laraine, also ended at around the same time and I was very lonely.

Soon afterwards I was shaken from my sadness by a phone call at college, or rather a message: 'Ring Chris Bonington.' This I did, warily conscious that a) it might be a practical joke or b) that I was about to be lumbered with something I'd regret. In the event it often seemed like a bit of both. Waiting while Louise, Chris's secretary, transferred me to the hot line and the man himself, I silently mouthed 'what ho's' into the phone.

'What ho,' it replied. 'Do you fancy a trip to China?'

'Yes,' I replied, conscious that Neil Murison, my head of department, was sitting opposite.

'What about your job?'

'No problem – I'll jack it in if I have to.'

Neil's face took on the look of weary resignation I'd seen so many times before as he realised that I was about to abscond yet again. Chris, meanwhile, was into overdrive with a barrage of logistics, dates and plans, to which I paid scant attention: with my hand over the phone I bounced around in the chair smothering giggles and making rude gestures at the complicated course timetable on the wall in front of me. '. . . of course, you'll have to have an interview with Michael Ward. Wear a suit and don't drop your aitches.' With this bit of helpful advice he rang off.

I had known Chris socially for several years and climbed with him in Britain on the odd occasion, particularly on his visit to Bristol lecturing, when he would kidnap me at short notice to climb in the Gorge. He is of course the 'Mr Big' of British climbing, but not an easy man to know, for his public and private persona change with bewildering rapidity. Occasionally he seems to find it difficult to differentiate between friendship and business relationships. Or to be more accurate he *does* differentiate them to such an extent that friendships have on occasion been sacrificed for the success of a venture. I sometimes think Chris would be surprised if he realised that there are many people who are not just very fond of him but also very loyal, despite his occasional cavalier treatment. He is undoubtedly the most enthusiastic climber I have ever met and never misses an opportunity to get out on the crags. His obvious love of climbing is his greatest strength for he can communicate it to the most blasé audience or uninformed reader of his books. His track record speaks for itself and I have always thought it a pity the way some younger climbers sneer at his high media profile and wheeling-dealing. His major sponsored successes on Annapurna and Everest have created the public awareness without which many smaller expeditions would never have got off the ground. Almost every British climber has a lot to thank Chris for, however indirectly.

What I had to thank Chris for was his appreciation of *The Bat* which he had seen at Kendal. Because of this I had drawn what I began to perceive as the short straw. I was asked to organise, direct and shoot a film, on my own, in a country about whose facilities we knew nothing, with a cast of high-powered climbers and scientists. The expedition was being led by Michael Ward, whose brainchild it largely was, and it had a scientific as well as mountaineering purpose. Michael is a leading figure in the field of high–altitude medicine. He was a doctor on the 1953 Everest expedition and is now a surgeon at a London hospital. He is very much an establishment figure.

In 1980 when China first opened its borders to foreign moun-taineers it was inevitable that Chris would get in on the act, and he and Michael had invited Al Rouse to join them on a reconnaissance expedition to Mount Kongur.

Al had burst into the British climbing scene in the early seventies.

For a short time he was probably the best rock climber in the country, then quickly moved on to master Scottish, Alpine and Andean climbing. His partnership with Rab Carrington came to fruition in their South American 'Supertrip' when they spent the best part of a year travelling from Patagonia to Peru, climbing sixteen routes, ten of which were new ones. In 1978, with Rab, Brian Hall and Roger Baxter-Jones he climbed Jannu alpine-style, a long, hard and committing route. I had got to know Al casually in the mid-seventies then much better when Laraine and I stayed with him and his French girlfriend Gwen in Chamonix for Christmas 1979.

In 1981 Kongur was one of the highest unclimbed mountains in the world at 7719 metres, and the only virgin peak on the small list of eight permitted mountains initially granted to foreigners by the Chinese Mountaineering Association. Set in Sinkiang Province, near the Russian border, Kongur was an unknown name in an unknown place. That was its main fascination for us, but also its handicap, for public interest starts and stops with mountains like Everest, the Matterhorn and the Eiger. Very occasionally new names join the list. Kongur's chances of doing this were scuppered by a throwaway line from Al at the end of their three months of exploration around the Kongur massif. When asked if the mountain would give any surprises the following year Al replied, 'Yes, we might have to use a rope!' With one sentence the mountain was dismissed as an easy snow plod and, despite the events of the following year, it never really achieved the status it deserved.

Al was now a Sheffield resident, suffering the trauma of Gwen's death in the winter of 1980 in a skiing accident in Chamonix. Between the Kongur recce and the main expedition in 1981 he was planning a winter attempt on the West Ridge of Everest. Joe Tasker, another Kongur team member, went on that trip as well. In February 1981 they returned emaciated and exhausted after a prolonged but unsuccessful attempt. They were in need of a long rest and I felt that neither of them ever really hit top form on Kongur. In particular Al seemed very susceptible to illness and had probably pushed himself too hard for too long.

Joe Tasker had risen to the top of the British Himalayan league with Peter Boardman in the mid-seventies. Together they had climbed the West Face of Changabang and the North Ridge of Kangchenjunga. Peter had climbed Everest South-West Face in 1975 when Mick Burke had disappeared near the summit. I got to know both of them during a hilarious week in 1978 when we drove to the Trento Film Festival together, stopping in Switzerland en route for a couple of climbs in

Peter Boardman (left) and Joe Tasker (above), one of the most formidable partnerships in British climbing.

Leysin, where Peter was about to become the new director of the International School of Mountaineering.

After Trento I got to know Joe better, though in many ways he was a very private person and I never felt completely relaxed in his company. Joe had been to a Catholic seminary, studying for the Jesuit priesthood and this, combined with his natural canny outlook on life, made him a man whose defences almost never dropped. I liked him and certainly grew to have enormous respect for his ability and willpower, but it would be untrue to pretend that I was ever as close to him as I was to Al or Paul or Mo. As for Peter, his life in Switzerland made him an increasingly remote figure, cut off from his own grassroots of British climbing. Peter was aware of this and conscious that he had ceased to be 'one of the lads'. He was essentially quite a shy person, though later I suspected that this was a bit of a front to hide behind, for in mountaineering terms Peter was ruthless, ferociously determined and very, very strong. There was no doubt that, with the possible exceptions of Doug Scott and Alex MacIntyre, Chris had made up the best available foursome to attempt Kongur lightweight and alpine-style.

The presence of four doctors ('One each,' said Al gleefully), a film-maker, David Wilson, political adviser to the Governor of Hong Kong who came along as an interpreter, plus a party of trekkers from our sponsors Jardine Matheson in Hong Kong, rather put paid to the idea of small is beautiful. Inside a large expedition a small one was always trying to get out.

After Chris's phone call came a long silence during which I began to doubt whether or not I was actually going to China. But a fortnight later in London, properly suited and tied, I met Michael Ward and Martin Henderson of Jardine Matheson. We were all identically dressed and all wore a navy blue tie with small white spots. I'd borrowed mine from one-time magazine proprietor and ex-army chef Nigel Gifford, and for a hideous moment thought it might be a club tie to which I had no right. There followed a strange interlude where I screened *Trango*, *The Bat* and *Barnaj* in a small viewing studio – always a gripping business with an audience of only two or three, when every fault seems all too obvious and the good bits, which you've seen hundreds of times anyway, fall flat. I found Michael almost a carica-ture of the successful London surgeon, formal, dry and precise. I wondered how we could possibly get on together on a long ex-pedition. In the event I couldn't have been more misled: once we left civilisation he underwent an almost miraculous transformation.

When I finally got my marching orders I was immediately plunged into the Bonington media machine of meetings, agents, contracts and receptions. A far cry from my departure at Sheffield Midland station for Delhi two years previously with two rucksacks, leaving a weeping girlfriend and an overdraft. Our send-off was rather more grandiose and took place at the Royal Geographical Society. After the usual platitudes and wishes of good luck we circulated uneasily through a crowded buffet grabbing drinks as quickly as decency permitted. I had brought with me an old friend, with the slightly improbable and certainly inappropriate name of Carole Innocent, to wave goodbye to at the airport, and it was she, with a shrewd kick to my ankle, who prevented my first major diplomatic faux pas before we even left London. I had been quizzed for about ten minutes by the inevitable photography enthusiast, a situation I always find embarrassing as they invariably know far more about cameras and equipment than I do. I thought his face vaguely familiar and should have cottoned on to his identity by the ease with which the gin and tonics were acquired and subsequently disappeared. As the conversation turned to jobs and I began to expound the folly of the education cuts, Carole butted in, half maiming me in the process and hissed in my ear that I was talking to Denis Thatcher!

It was difficult to dissociate him from his *Private Eye* image when he observed, 'At least China's got decent khazis these days.' Al, trying to make conversation, remarked that he must have to do a lot of travelling himself. 'Yes. Off to Mexico next month for some binge' – this was in fact a Third World conference – 'rich versus the poor.' On hearing that we were flying out in the midst of an aircraft controllers' dispute he snorted, 'It's about time those bounders did an honest day's work!' But it was hard not to like him, and he did seem genuinely interested in the expedition. So much so that months later we found ourselves ushered through the most famous doorway in Britain and lavishly entertained for two short but enjoyable hours before being smoothly ejected into Downing Street once more, wondering if we had dreamed the whole thing.

Before we left London, Sir Douglas Busk, chairman of the Mount Everest Foundation, wished us luck and parted with the immortal line – 'If you need any help, send me a telegram.' Two months later Al Rouse suggested its contents: 'Stuck in snow coffins 4 nights 7000 metres. Bad storm no food. Please advise.'

The almost empty British Airways 747 touched down in what was only then beginning to be called Beijing and disgorged a gang of jet-lagged, hung-over insomniacs masquerading as an expedition, who had availed themselves of free booze all the way from Heathrow. Ten years on it is curious to recall just how differently China struck us in comparison with the other Asian countries we were more familiar with. Now of course Beijing has as much media coverage as anywhere else in the world, most recently in the appalling and nauseating massacre of student protesters. But to us in 1981, driving from the modern airport to the city, everything was new, even if it was all pretty drab. Thousands of cyclists thronged the roads. On street corners and in cafés excited groups played card games with much gesticulation of triumph or despair. Single-storey mud houses or blocks of flats seemed unnaturally dull until I realised that in communist China there was no advertising to speak of. Strange that most hoardings and posters are eyesores yet, without them, urban landscapes are deprived of much colour and life.

The overriding feeling I remember was one of how absolutely 'foreign' it all was. Not understanding a word of Chinese, not recognising a single European word and realising that, unlike in Pakistan, Nepal and India, speaking English was of no use whatsoever, it was impossible to do more than gawp at everything. I found this very disturbing for the first few days, despite the overwhelming politeness and attention we were paid, for Jardine Matheson, the great trading company of Hong Kong, had major business interests in Beijing, so we were a hugely privileged group.

Other British expeditions since, without such generous sponsorship and high-level contacts, have had very different experiences. The main problem is of course money. Expeditions to China pay ludicrously over-the-top rates for anything and everything, but as one official put it bluntly, 'We have something you want: you must pay what we ask. If you don't pay, you don't get it.' There is little scope for the bartering and corner-cutting that is the norm in Pakistan, India and Nepal, and often the Chinese simply don't provide the services promised and paid for. In 1981, however, we were blissfully spared all these problems and the whole expedition ran like clockwork from the first day to the last; apart from the bits we managed to cock up ourselves.

Official limos, or 'rimos' as Al had learned to call them the previous year, whisked us around the Forbidden City, the Ming Tombs and the Great Wall to get our obligatory ticks in the Great Places of the World list. The same happened in Urumchi and Kashgar when we reached Sinkiang Province, but at least here we had more time to explore on our own. We noticed a huge change in our reception once away from Chinese officialdom. Indifference and suspicion gave way to smiles and overwhelming curiosity.

In the early days of the expedition we were very conscious of the presence of our sponsors, for the trekking party which was accompanying us to Base Camp included the chairman of Jardine Matheson, David Newbigging, his wife Carolyn, and some of their friends and colleagues. Chris in particular was eager to give a good impression. I was seeing him 'at work' for the first time and there is no doubt that expeditions, which most of us treat as wonderful, glorified holidays until Base Camp is reached , are used by Chris as valuable periods of time to work flat out on logistics, news reports, postcard signings, meetings and a thousand other chores.

He was keen I should film anything and everything so that David Newbigging could see I was doing the job his company was paying for, and I grew to resent a variety of well-meaning suggestions, not just from Chris but from almost all the team. Whenever I set up formal shots on the big tripod in the cities I was quite literally overcome with hundreds of curious spectators flocking in front of the lens. I had already shot a lot of film, mostly hand-held, and sometimes even by just walking alone with the running camera held by my side, so difficult was it to get natural shots.

There was a strong undercurrent of competition in our team that manifested itself in different forms. Running was one. Chris, Pete Boardman and Charlie Clarke were all dedicated joggers and Martin Henderson of Jardine Matheson was an ex-university runner, who knocked spots off the others. I found (and still do, despite years of flirting with the activity) that whereas jogging undoubtedly gets you fit for jogging, it doesn't do much for high-altitude mountaineering which mainly consists of walking slowly uphill with a heavy load on your back.

Al Rouse was even more extreme in his views, because he couldn't run anyway, due to chronic ankle troubles caused by at least three accidents over the years. He recounted with satisfaction that a marathon runner he had guided in the States was a disaster as he was trained to perform for a mere two or three hours. On a big rock climb he became physically and psychologically exhausted after this time had elapsed. So Al and I resisted invitations to join the joggers and hid in Joe's bedroom like naughty schoolchildren, paying court to the bedridden malingerer. The doctors were convinced that Joe had got an intestinal worm, which he hadn't, but he did not argue as he was correcting the proofs of his new book and had no time to spend on sightseeing or jogging. The runners meanwhile insisted on running around the streets of Kashgar in blistering heat, to the utter amazement of the inhabitants who, as H. W. Tilman had noticed years before, regard it as exceedingly bad form so much as to cross the street on foot if it is possible to ride across on a horse.

One day we were taken to the old British consulate where Eric Shipton had served a term as consul after the Second World War. Set outside Kashgar on a slight hill, it should have commanded a magnificent view, for behind the city was rumoured to be a distant sight of the Chinese Pamirs, even Kongur itself. But throughout our stay there was little or no visibility through the layer of sandy haze that hung over the city and desert. The consulate, long since abandoned, is now a truck drivers' hostel and, although it was obviously an elegant building, gave little inkling of its former grandeur. But I dutifully filmed inside and out without much clear idea of how to use the scene in a documentary film. The story of Shipton's tenure was interesting but visually it was less than riveting. We went on to visit a primary school which seemed even less promising. But here, to my increasing frustration, was a fantastic display of folk dancing and music. Children in bright make-up and traditional dress paraded in front of us to

the accompaniment of violins and drums. And I had just run out of
film! I returned dolefully to the hotel and inevitably bumped into
Chris who tersely advised me to get my act together. Knowing that
this time he was right didn't help.

During our days in Kashgar I shared a hotel room with Al Rouse
and from then on we tended to stick together, sharing a kind of anti-
establishment humour at the expense of the more excessively pomp-
ous pronouncements of Chris and Michael, who could reduce us to
helpless mirth at some of their better efforts. Once I reminisced with
Chris about a classic article in *Mountain* magazine by Mike
Thompson, called 'Out With the Boys Again'. This poked fun at
Chris's leadership on the 1975 Everest South-West Face expedition.

I reminded Chris of one of its best lines: '"'Welcome aboard,' said
our leader, using the terminology of the only one of the armed forces
that he hadn't been a member of.'"'

Chris looked vaguely puzzled. 'I'm sure I didn't really say that –
Mike was obviously writing metaphorically – all I was trying to do
was keep the ship on an even keel!'

Michael Ward had boarded the plane at Heathrow in a suit but as
soon as we took off he discarded his tie and with it the trappings of
civilisation. Relaxed, he told with glee stories of surgical horrors and
announced with relish to Joe Tasker, 'My dear chap, I'll put my hands
anywhere so long as I am wearing rubber gloves!' He once summed up
the medical profession with grim humour. 'There are only two kinds
of illness, one you recover from and one you die from. Our role is
purely peripheral.'

The morning we left Kashgar we awoke at six to find that the haze
had dispersed. On the horizon a huge, white wall reared up. Even at
this distance the mountains seemed vast and indeed the height difference is over 5000 metres. Chris pointed out Kongur and I climbed
aboard our minibus with some foreboding. All morning we drove
towards the great white barrier, which, as the dust rose, seemed to be
suspended higher and higher above us. But this was not 'our' side of
the mountain; we were approaching Kongur from the north. We
entered the Gez Gorge up which traces of the old Silk Road could still
be seen and slowly in the midday heat ground our way up a never-
ending series of dirt hairpins. This was actually the Karakoram
Highway and it was curious to think that if we carried on driving we
would end up in Gilgit in Pakistan. At last the top of the gorge was
reached and the view opened up. Only occasionally have I been so
aware of such vast open spaces and huge skies. A great sandy plain
stretched away into high sand dunes, incongruously spattered with

fresh snow. Behind them lay rounded black mountains that seemed to stretch away for ever towards Russia in the west. In the foreground was a herd of wild horses. We just had time for a quick photograph before they shied away in alarm. Above us the intensely blue sky had an almost oppressive reality. Back in the minibus we drove the last miles up to the Karakol Lakes, two superb stretches of water that reflected the bulk of Muztagh Ata, a gently angled mountain of 7456 metres. But where had Kongur gone?

We sat on the cropped grass by the lakeside waiting for the lorry of equipment to arrive and gazed around, slightly bemused to be suddenly transported to 3000 metres. Away to the north was a long, seemingly unbroken ridge. Behind it, jutting into the clouds and trailing a banner of wind-driven snow, was a steep black cone, the summit pyramid of Kongur – it looked high, cold and remote.

'I thought you said this was supposed to be a walk.' Pete sounded aggrieved with Al. 'It looks bloody big and serious to me.'

With the arrival of all our kit we set about erecting a big frame tent, or rather the others did while I filmed the fiasco. Being climbers, no one bothered to read the instructions and when they at last realised that they had got to, they couldn't understand them. Eventually the tall, earnest and bespectacled figure of Martin Henderson took over command and within minutes the tent was up. I wondered what the other Jardine personnel thought as we failed a test that a group of Girl Guides would have passed with ease.

Next morning we awoke to a sharp frost, which quickly melted, and a glorious day. I carted the camera and tripod to the other side of an inlet facing the tents and filmed a staggeringly beautiful set of mountain reflections. Brown side-lit hills, the white Mustagh Ata and the orange and blue tents against an azure sky were perfectly mirrored in the flat calm of the Karakol Lakes.

We were to spend the best part of a week at the lakes. While small groups trekked to small surrounding peaks for a bit of early acclimatisation and exercise, I made the first serious onslaught on the film. Because of this I only managed to gain altitude once during the week, about which more anon, for I was engaged in the game of 'Hunt the Kirghiz'. This was to be a highlight of the film for the Kirghiz tribe are colourful nomads who formerly wandered at will between China, Russia and Afghanistan. They are great horsemen and their camps are famous for their *yurts*, ornate felt tents furnished with colourful rugs and carpets. Chris, Michael and even Al had waxed eloquent about the need to film them. But unlike last year, when there had been several encampments near the lakes, they were now conspicuous by their absence. Being nomads they were apparently being nomadic which I thought seemed fair enough, but everyone else appeared to be slightly aggrieved that there was no one around to stare at (or be stared at by).

After a few days in which I circumnavigated the lakes, got chased into them by a dog and filmed the others crossing a stream in a small inflatable dinghy, my luck changed. Someone had spotted a Kirghiz encampment about a mile away. I persuaded Al Rouse to be sound recordist for the day and we set out, wondering what my reactions would be if a couple of foreigners came barging into my Bristol flat merely to record the fact that I existed.

Our arrival was heralded by the frantic barking of three or four large, unpleasant dogs. Eventually their owners managed to restrain them from ripping out our throats. I was pleased to see that they maintained a healthy respect for the beasts and were quite relieved themselves when the dogs were tethered, still growling horribly, out of harm's way. With great ceremony we were ushered into the biggest of three *yurts* and plied with yoghurt and *nan* bread until it was in danger of coming out of our ears. The children were beautifully dressed with highly decorated scarves, ornate earrings and necklaces. One, about fifteen, was very aware of her good looks and flirted outrageously, smiling and winking in a most disturbing way. Her elder sister looked very disapproving.

As we had absolutely no common language, conversation consisted of long silences broken occasionally by well-meaning grunts of approval on both sides. Perhaps language evolved simply out of embarrassment? At last, jaws aching with constant smiling, I pointed to the movie camera. Instantly everyone struck formal poses that transformed the scene to a Victorian photograph. I tried to explain, with desperate recourse to mime, that this was movie film, but to no avail. The Kirghiz obviously hoped that I was using an elaborate Polaroid camera and were disappointed that they couldn't instantly watch the exposed film unwind from the magazine. I could film whatever I wanted and after half an hour or so we left well satisfied. But I was conscious that we had brought nothing for them and had taken more. I need not have worried, for the following morning what appeared to be the entire Kirghiz tribe turned up to have their photographs taken properly on the one Polaroid camera that Chris had had the foresight to bring for just such an eventuality.

Another day Al suggested a training walk towards Base Camp about seven miles away up gentle rolling hillsides of baked mud, scrub and boulders. Between us and the first incline was the Konsiver River. This had given Chris and our Chinese Liaison Officer, Liu Dayi, a near-terminal accident the previous year. Attempting to ford it in spate they had both been swept away and were lucky to survive. Chris was obviously badly shaken by the affair and we all had our own memories of river crossings that had nearly gone wrong.

Charlie Clarke had come up with the idea of a rubber dinghy that could be attached to a pulley system, and a whole day had been spent constructing a ropeway, using expansion bolts drilled into boulders on each side of the river to anchor the ropes. There was only one snag, which was the water level, which at this time of the year was only the merest trickle.

Al was the lightest member of the team and I was the heaviest. Both of us had a healthy mistrust of boats. These two factors combined on our training walk when a humiliating little episode (luckily not witnessed by anyone else) caused us to capsize and abandon ship in almost six inches of water. Panic-stricken we paddled ashore from the shipwreck, risking hypothermia of the ankles. The rest of the walk passed off uneventfully and we dropped a couple of tents just below the site of Base Camp to descend leisurely and well content to the lakes to be in good time for dinner. We ignored the dinghy on our return and waded easily across the river.

It had been a good day and one in which I could relax in Al's company. Both of us felt that there was too much point-scoring within the group (though Al himself was a past master at doing this) and that everyone was being unnecessarily serious. In Kashgar for instance, Pete and Joe had hardly left the hotel, Joe because he was correcting proofs and Pete because he was busy reading up the history of the area for the forthcoming expedition book. I had been amazed that their interests seemed so academic and that Pete in particular didn't appear to be very curious about the reality in which he found himself. I am sure Pete felt that Al and I were too flippant and too concerned with simply enjoying ourselves. I couldn't see what was wrong with that. Al and I were being exposed for the first time to a level of professional mountaineering that gave us grave misgivings as to whether it was worth getting so intense about.

At last the time had come to move the whole circus up to Base Camp. This necessitated the use of both yaks and camels. We were also taking a flock of seven sheep with us (vegetarians please ignore the reason for this) and I filmed with some amusement Michael Ward at the helm of the dinghy, ferrying them one by one across the river – surely a first for a London surgeon.

Late next morning we arrived at Base Camp amongst scenes of spectacular chaos as yaks were unloaded randomly, leaving loads scattered over a wide area. Chris decided (with good reason) that he had been giving me a rather hard time recently and helped me put up my tent, apologising for his earlier bad temper. Suddenly I warmed to his company and appreciated his concern, though I couldn't help wishing he wouldn't do it in the first place.

Our Base Camp was an attractive spot, except that there was no view to speak of. Kongur remained hidden by a much smaller peak above us, and the great vista down to the Lakes could only be seen by visiting our lavatory – an old-fashioned wooden thunderbox. Not for nothing was it called 'The Loo with a View'. We were camped on grass and off the glacier, a most important consideration, as it enabled us all to relax and unwind when off the mountain, without the constant stress of living on a glacier which is the case at K2 and many other Himalayan base camps.

Before they left for home our trekking party were to take in one of the small peaks surrounding Base Camp, guided by the Gang of Four, as I had labelled the climbing team. My enviable if less onerous duty was to escort Carolyn Newbigging for a gentle walk across the glacier leading to the foot of the easy-looking mountain that had been selected for the outing. Carolyn was the only woman on the expedition. We all thought she was wonderful: sympathetic, easy to talk to and totally adjusted to the unusual situation she found herself in, a far cry from the opulent lifestyle of one of Hong Kong society's leading ladies. Despite my humble duty for the day, I suspected that some of the others would have swapped roles quite willingly.

Together with Tom Harley, another of the Jardine executives, we set off for our not too strenuous outing over the dry but convoluted lower reaches of the Koksel Glacier, marvelling at some fantastic towers and pinnacles of green ice. Carolyn adopted a strange and, I have to say, wholly feminine approach to mountain travel by running very fast ('before I get too out of breath') for short distances, then sitting down to wait for Tom and me to catch up. I adopted the Mo Anthoine adage which said that if you can't smoke and walk uphill at the same time you are going too fast. This Tom appreciated almost as much as my reporting of another of Mo's observations, which was that if God had wanted us to jog he wouldn't have given us the wit to invent the motorcar.

On the far side of the glacier we were surprised to see Al returning down the lower slopes of the mountain. He was full of cold and flu and offered to take over my onerous duties. I was quite disappointed to relinquish them. Carolyn, despite referring to me as nanny whenever I offered her any advice, was a lot more attractive than the boring-

A foreshortened view up the couloir to the Trango Tower at a moment when it was not raining rocks as big as buses.

Mo Anthoine fighting his way up the final hard chimneys.

The south summit of Barnaj II in a rare spell of fine weather.
Tony Riley leading an ice pitch on the second Barnaj expedition.

Filming The Bat: *above, Rab Carrington traverses towards the Hoodie Groove; below, Brian Hall in mid-fall, a still from the film.*

Our first view of Kongur and its elusive summit pyramid.
Dawn on the South Ridge from the summit of the Pimple.

Halfway up 450 feet of sandstone and regurgitated fulmars' breakfast, Paul Nunn pauses to offer me some advice on the Old Man of Hoy. Phil Kershaw waits below.

Al Rouse teetering up the first ascent of Act of Faith (E3 6b), Ashop Edge, Kinder North, June 1985.

Geoff Tier on the East Ridge of Palomani Tranca.
A snowstorm over pre-Inca tombs, Lake Titicaca.

The epitome of sea-cliff climbing, the author on Lundy granite, 1980.

Henry Barber leads the Rasp, Higgar Tor, Derbyshire, seconded by Cathy Woodhead.

Pete Whillance and Ian McMullan finishing the hardest section on the first ascent of Conachair on St Kilda.

looking mounds of rotten rock and scree that Al had just descended. But I could see his point when he told me I would earn some brownie points by making a token effort to acclimatise. So I set off, head down and taking small steps. Unladen, I gained height remarkably easily. After an hour or two I reached a slight narrowing of the ridge and saw several dark shapes ahead of me in the blowing cloud that streamed off the top hundred metres or so of the mountain. I could hardly believe it. It was the others moving slowly upwards just below the summit. I seemed to be catching them up for now I was following good tracks in knee-deep snow that must have cost quite a lot of effort in trail breaking.

I have to admit I was excited. Though no more than a walk the peak was a respectable 5500 metres, not bad after only ten days or so from sea level. As I approached the top I was breathing hard from more than simple exertion. Quite unexpectedly I was about to climb a mountain – the first time ever, on an expedition, and a virgin peak to boot! Hood up and facing into the teeth of the wind, I staggered up the last few feet to join the throng. 'Who are you?' yelled someone.

The news that it was Jim was greeted less than ecstatically, I thought, as I tried to light a cigarette between blasts of spindrift. I was supposed to be the unfit one. Unlike our trekkers, I had not spent the last months jogging up and down the hills of Hong Kong. So maybe my joining them at their moment of triumph slightly detracted from their sense of achievement. Bugger it, never mind, it certainly didn't detract from mine and I revelled in the simple joy of standing looking at what wasn't a very good view of a cloud-covered Kongur.

9

WAITING FOR THE CLIMBERS

ONCE THE trekking team departed the atmosphere both relaxed and became more focused on the job in hand. Yet within a couple of days the expedition reached its low point. Chris, who with Joe Tasker had set out to establish an Advance Base Camp in the huge glacial Koksel Basin, returned having picked up Al's flu virus. This rapidly turned into pneumonia. In sustained bad weather our spirits fell as Chris seemed to be out of it completely. Seeing him tottering round Base Camp ashen-faced and coughing horribly I imagined he would take no further part in the expedition. Pete, Joe and Al, who was recovering somewhat, left to explore the lower reaches of the South Ridge of Kongur, which rose in steps from the Koksel Col. I accompanied them as far as Advance Base and teamed up with David Wilson, our interpreter. David was a keen fell runner and mountain explorer, though he had not done much serious mountaineering. He had already proved to be an invaluable addition to the team, a widely read Chinese scholar with more knowledge of the country in his little finger than the rest of us combined. He was incredibly fit and enthusiastic and it seemed a good idea for us to work together to compensate for my sloth and indecision. At the Karakol Lakes David had done a lot of running and Al had fantasised that, far from being a political adviser for the Hong Kong government, he was actually a Russian spy – returning over the border to inform his masters from Moscow of the capitalist intruders! Certainly David's urbane manners and rather dashing appearance had a touch of the James Bond, but he took Al's jibes in good part, the best being, 'That's a nice watch, David. Does it take good pictures?'

Our pairing was the subject for some mirth, as in appearance and attitude we could hardly have been more different, but we actually got

David Wilson with whom I worked out how to share a tent.

on extremely well and David's tolerance for my uncouth habits had certainly earned my profound respect. On our first foray to Advance Base I had, as usual, been violently sick in the middle of the night. This seems to occur every time I spend my first night above 5500 metres and came as no surprise to me. David had endured the event in the confines of a tiny Salewa tent and next day repitched it. Peter Boardman asked him why, to which David replied it was to enable me to be sick out of the other side the following night. But David's major cross to bear was the fact that I smoked heavily and he didn't. In an effort to compromise I smoked with my head out of the tent and realised that my dedication to nicotine had given me frost-numbed fingers in the cigarette-holding hand. However, David did have one habit that I also found disgusting, and that was the ability to eat a huge breakfast and consume chocolate at will. At any altitude my appetite disappears and in the mornings I can only cope with sweet tea (plus the inevitable cigarette). David's early morning feasts were carried out in secrecy at the far end of the tent while I determinedly laid a smoke-screen at the other.

While Pete and Joe were pushing their first foray up and over the first little summit of the South Ridge, known from the reconnaissance as the Pimple, Al, still weak and coughing violently, only went as far as the Koksel Col. At 5700 metres this seemed a realistic objective for us as well, and on a bitingly cold day with a whipping wind blowing clouds of spindrift high in the air, David and I breasted the last, long, easy slopes to the col, getting a superb view of dozens of unnamed, unclimbed mountains on the eastern side. Many of them, I have to say, looked more interesting than Kongur, if a bit lower.

Later that day I filmed and photographed Pete and Joe as they climbed over the Pimple. With a big telephoto lens from Advance Base I could just pick them out at a distance of around three miles. When contrasted with the whole length of the South Ridge, it was perhaps the best and clearest indication of scale I have ever seen in the mountains and one that works well in lectures where it is always desperately difficult to illustrate just how huge mountains are. Pete and Joe returned in the evening, trudging into camp at a disconcertingly fast pace considering how tired they said they felt. Al, probably disappointed at his own weakness, set to, cooking and brewing for them as they unwound.

It was interesting being a spectator at Advance Base and watching the three of them jockeying for position. There was no doubt in my mind that physically Pete was by far and away the strongest. He was also the most forceful: now in the environment he loved, his confidence, knowledge and ability emerged. Gone was the slightly 'little boy lost' image he portrayed in Britain, to be replaced by the sort of decisive competence one would expect of the high-powered executives who had so recently returned to Hong Kong. Joe, on the other hand, was still very much the Joe of sea level. Overtly lazy (he always did his damnedest to avoid camp chores of any kind) and laid back, there was no mistaking his ruthless ambition and obsessive determination to keep up with Pete. They had, over the years, developed a strange relationship: like an old married couple, nagging and criticising each other and arguing relentlessly over trivial issues. Joe in particular never gave way, and though Pete was physically much the stronger of the two, I suspected that if willpower alone was what got you up mountains that Joe was almost his equal.

Al, normally so voluble and extrovert, became more and more uncertain of himself and less and less assertive as the trip progressed.

He had got on extremely well with Chris and Michael the previous year but now I saw him being edged down the pecking order by Pete and Joe, who together were a formidable couple to compete with. Al had adopted the most extreme ethical stance in his adherence to alpine-style climbing. This was a bit pointless on an expedition that had already shown itself to be open to all kinds of not too significant compromise in this respect. By sticking to his moral guns Al undoubtedly alienated himself somewhat, particularly as he couldn't back up his views with his own performance, which remained slightly below par for the whole expedition.

Apart from his principles, Al also had two practical differences of opinion with the others, first over what route should be attempted and second in his conviction of the superiority of snow holes over tents. In the end events proved him right on both counts, which didn't make relationships any easier, particularly with Pete with whom there was a definite feeling of rivalry. At home, Al was undoubtedly better known than Pete as a brilliant rock climber and had received (perhaps squandered) a Cambridge University education. Pete, who had graduated from Nottingham University, seemed to feel that Al was a slightly mercurial and insubstantial figure and was continually irritated by Al's never-ending ability, even if almost inaudible with his sore throat, to argue and score points on a wide variety of topics, many of which I had long since learned to take with a pinch of salt. Although these differences never developed into anything worse, there was certainly a degree of tension between them that Al generally seemed completely unaware of. I hoped for Al's sake that Chris recovered sufficiently to climb. The balance would then be restored somewhat, for three was in any case a very awkward number to climb together.

The day after Pete and Joe's explorations, we descended to Base Camp for a rest and to see how well Chris was recovering. On our return we were plunged into two very different worlds. One was of sheer pampered luxury. Meals, cooked by Wang, one of our smiling, ever cheerful Chinese staff, were varied, delicious, and of fantastic ingenuity. I have never before or since had so many different dishes to choose from on an expedition. There was also a 'goody' box of sweet and savoury snacks that were available at any time of day or night, as were unlimited supplies of White Horse whisky. This was supplied in plastic bottles that were being tested by the makers for use on aircraft due to their considerable saving in weight. It was also an advantage for us, and one that even Al could approve of in his continuing quest to make his rucksack as light as possible.

The other world was of high-altitude medicine. Being a late arrival on the Kongur expedition, I had mercifully avoided all the pre-expedition medical tests, so as there was no pre-expedition data to compare me with, the doctors left me alone most of the time and devoted their energies to the Gang of Four. But no one was excused the worst ritual of all: blood tests. These were carried out by Edward Williams, normally the most gentle, mild-mannered of men, in whose company one instantly felt relaxed, trusting and at ease. Put a hypo-dermic syringe in his hand, however, and Edward would become transformed. Vampire-like, with bloodshot eyes, dripping fangs and his Helly Hansen polar jacket worn as a cloak, he would pursue his innocent victims around Base Camp until he could suck out what little blood was left in our veins. By this time it had been reduced to a treacly consistency due to altitude and was horribly painful to extract. Then he would whisk the results up in a glorified Kenwood mixer and deposit what looked like a strawberry milk-shake in a giant thermos flask that emitted Frankenstein tendrils of ice-cold vapour. As the expedition progressed I found myself spending longer and longer periods at Advance Base Camp and, when I did go down, feigned illness of one sort or another in which case all the doctors left me severely alone.

Chris, who had overdone this particular gambit with his pneu-monia, was making a miraculously quick recovery. I have to admit that Charlie Clarke was also instrumental in this. But he was still not fit enough for a summit bid and the others felt they were not sufficiently acclimatised either. So they decided on another extensive foray above Advance Base. This suited me for, slowly, with the dubious help of two Chinese porters (or 'assistants' as the Chinese insisted they be called) I was getting everything I needed up to Advance Base and beyond. Edward Williams very kindly offered to help cart the big tripod all the way to the Koksel Col in exchange for a pint or so of my blood should I ever be passing his tent at Base Camp. I am afraid he will never forget the herculean effort necessary to wade through thigh-deep powder snow to the Col. But it was an invaluable carry and significantly improved the long shots I needed higher up the mountain.

I was now ready to film the ascent of the South Ridge of Kongur and was relieved when after yet another rest at Base Camp, it was decided to go for the Ridge rather than the easier angled and featureless South-West Rib that Al had favoured. The South Ridge was undoubtedly more photogenic and I was hoping to pitch a tent on or near the summit of the Pimple from which I hoped I would get good views of the four climbers on the upper section of the Ridge.

Charlie Clarke, who seemed to have increasing trouble acclimatising, accompanied David Wilson and me to Advance Base to lend a hand in getting us established on the Pimple. But he was so ill during the night that he couldn't set out for the Col next morning. So I had to do a quick pruning of camera gear until David and I could manage everything on our own. Then, after a stormy night on the Koksel Col, the next day dawned with half a gale blasting across the Col. It was bitterly cold and, after a long lie-in, listening to the wind cracking against the walls of the tiny two-man Limpet tent, I took it upon myself to postpone our departure.

This was a difficult decision. David was keen to press on but I felt responsible for our mini-expedition. If, through my misjudgment, we got ourselves into trouble, Chris and the lads would not thank us if their attempt turned into a rescue or worse. Though the Pimple didn't seem to offer much difficulty, it was steep enough for us to rope up and climb in pitches at least for its initial rocky section.

The following morning brought better weather and also Chris, Al, Pete and Joe, who stomped up to the Col looking fit and determined, and incidentally providing some of the best footage I shot on the entire expedition. They soon disappeared from view, leaving us with our rucksack full of cameras, film and tents, floundering painfully uphill in their footsteps.

Above was a stretch of easy ice climbing, no more than Scottish Grade II or III. Here, at around 6000 metres, it was well worth roping up and moving one at a time. Faced with real climbing, I got a surge of enthusiasm and really enjoyed the next three or four pitches, which took us to easy ground and the resumption of the desperate snow-flogging that had been the norm for so much of the whole expedition. The buzz of excitement faded and I suddenly felt terribly tired. David pulled ahead and I followed slowly in his tracks. Suddenly there was a shout from above. It was Joe, descending to give David Wilson a letter to post to Maria, his girlfriend. David was planning to descend to Base Camp after our little outing while I hoped to stay at Advance Base to film the conquering heroes on their return. Joe, spotting me in, if not extremis, then not far from it, descended and offered to carry my sack to the top of the Pimple, a kind and very helpful gesture. Without its weight I could carry on at a slightly faster speed and at last we breasted the final slopes to arrive on the rounded summit, and the most exposed campsite in Central Asia.

Joe pressed quickly on to rejoin the other three, preparing to camp about 300 metres along the South Ridge, which fell away below us, then gradually regained height once more before the long steep upper slopes. We were now at around 6200 metres, a personal best for me at the time. I was very tired and cold and unable to do much more than act as ballast inside the tent as David struggled to pitch it. Once it was up and we had got a brew on I felt much better but I was worried at my lack of stamina after an average, but not excessively long, day. It took some time to get sorted and I had to sleep with the Scoopic cine camera in my sleeping-bag to stop it freezing up. I wanted to be able to start filming at first light and realised that with luck I would get some really good views the next day. The wind had dropped to almost nothing for about the first time since our arrival a month ago. The temperature also dropped to minus nothing – one of the coldest nights of my life.

At first light I carefully unzipped the tent door, trying to stop a thick crust of hoar frost falling on our sleeping-bags, and peered out to a stunning dawn. The first low rays of sun were shining from below on to the east-facing ice flutings of the ridge ahead. Behind, the summit cone of Kongur, invisible since we had left the Karakol Lakes, was also dramatically illuminated against a still-dark sky. A stray shaft of sunshine just lit the two tiny orange tents. Hastily, with frozen fingers, I struggled with the camera and tripod to capture the magic effects before the sun rose any higher and to my relief managed to shoot what eventually became the title shot of the film. I also grabbed a few still photographs before crawling back into my sleeping-bag. Periodically I glanced out to see if the Gang of Four were up and about but it was not until almost eleven a.m. that they left the tents. As this was exactly the time that David and I had set off the day before I allowed myself a wry smile. They had obviously found it just as cold as we had.

All day the four tiny dots gained height painfully slowly on the great snow ridge in front of us. We had a grandstand view and with the zoom lens of the movie camera it was possible once more to show the scale of our surroundings. But the most impressive sight was not the Ridge and the climbers, nor even the summit of Kongur, but the views away from the mountain. Far below, and now about twelve miles away, the Karakol Lakes gleamed a bright turquoise. Behind, the brown and purple hills etched with streaks of dirty dust-covered snow stretched away to the Russian border in the west and to Afghanistan in the south. Range upon range of them, inhabited presumably by a mere handful of Kirghiz, but otherwise unexplored. It was a sight I shall never forget. In its wild desolation it remains the single most haunting view I have ever seen. Though there was none of the dramatic mountain architecture of the Karakoram, or a range of famous names as in the Everest region, there was a feeling of unlimited space and a timeless grandeur that in my slightly euphoric state I found quite moving. Having a whole day to spend on a summit, albeit a minor one, was a unique experience for David and me.

Late in the afternoon grey clouds started drifting across the South Ridge. The four dots, now within striking distance of the top of the Ridge, were spread unevenly; a figure I guessed correctly was Pete drew ahead but the other three stayed close together, following in his footsteps. It was the last we were to see of them for four days. Puffs of cloud swirled up from below us and blotted out the view. There was no point in stopping here for another day, for the figures would almost certainly remain out of sight.

Next morning we descended to the Col. David was full of energy and determined to get all the way down to Base Camp that day, in order to deliver the letters and news film for ITN in London. I would stay at Advance Base with Michael Ward and wait to meet the Gang of Four, whom we assumed would be returning triumphant in a couple of days or so.

At Advance Base it was hard to imagine what could be going on high above us. The weather had deteriorated somewhat but was nowhere near as bad or as cold as it had been. Michael and I were cautiously optimistic. Three long days passed and then we spotted them, slowly descending the long, easy-angled snow slopes of the South-West Rib. I was keen to film them as they arrived in camp, so Michael left to meet them, taking some cold drinks with him. Impatiently, I watched the tiny figures converge, stop, and then set off for the last mile or so back across the Koksel Basin. Afternoon sunshine lit up the snow as the figures took shape. Foreshortened, they moved around the camera frame, never appearing to get nearer. It was impossible to see their expressions behind their sunglasses. They looked tired.

Silently they arrived, dragging their feet through the soft snow. 'Sorry, Jim, we didn't do it.' A flat statement of fact suddenly dashed my fantasies of a triumphant return to the fleshpots of Hong Kong, gallons of ice-cold beer, soft sheets and phone calls home. We would be here for at least another fortnight. Gloomily I completed a couple of shots of four climbers drinking endless brews of tea and then listened to their story.

'It was a bit of a downer,' Al said later. 'Really we weren't even on the right mountain – there was a huge gap between us and the summit pyramid. It looked hard, long and steep – a bit like Gasherbrum IV' (one of the most beautiful and difficult Karakoram mountains).

To make matters worse they weren't too sure how to get across to the foot of the summit pyramid and at one stage Al had consulted the glossy expedition brochure to try to make sense of the photographs taken the previous year. The dotted lines so confidently plotted in Britain seemed to be a trifle optimistic, and took no account of the 150-metre drop to the knife-edged ridge leading to the foot of the final pyramid. They had dug a big snow hole just before the start of the ridge and next day set out on a rather forlorn summit bid. Difficult climbing up, over and round gendarmes and along the narrow, tottering crest of the ridge had taken hours. There was no chance of completing the climb that day and they were almost out of food and gas. They had no real choice but to descend, though Pete, as usual the driving force, wanted to carry on. All four were very tired, but I was impressed by their determination to have another go, and wondered how many other expeditions would have packed up at this point. Obviously they needed a proper rest and the following morning we descended to the luxury of Base Camp, blood tests and all.

After only three days the Gang of Four set off once more. I had persuaded Joe to carry an Autoload camera and eight cartridges of film that the team shared between them. Joe was a quick and enthusiastic learner and even took a tiny monopod mount which screwed on to his ice axe so that he could keep the camera steady. I urged him to keep it simple and make the shots too long rather than too short. I hoped that with luck he could bring back a couple of minutes' invaluable footage of the upper part of the mountain.

Michael Ward and I re-established ourselves at Advance Base to await their return once more. We were there for a week, during which time a major storm hit the mountain. Snow fell continuously and with no word from above we spent hours theorising about what might have happened and working out a hypothetical schedule of their movements, which in the event proved to be surprisingly accurate.

During the long days of waiting I got to know Michael better than I ever imagined possible when I first met him in London months before. He had a strong interest in the arts and an extremely inquisitive mind, full of probing and intelligent questions. I was able to bullshit to my heart's content about subjects I rarely discussed on expeditions. In exchange Michael, who was in his youth a brilliant rock climber and mountaineer, regaled me with stories of climbing in Britain with legendary names like W. H. Murray and Menlove Edwards. Michael had been a member of the famous Everest reconnaissance in 1951 when the Icefall was explored and the route through the Western Cwm, the Lhotse Face and the South Col was seen to be feasible. Then in 1953 he was one of two doctors on Hunt's successful expedition. Michael told with relish of past feuds and rivalries, of obscure scandals and little-known events. It was an age of mountaineering I knew little about apart from my favourite childhood mountaineering book, *South Col*. Now here was the first-hand story from one of the participants.

Michael had rarely been on an expedition without the presence of Sherpas to look after the sahibs. Consequently he had the greatest trouble with even the simplest domestic chores. Despite his manual dexterity as a surgeon, he never managed to master the art of striking a match, let alone producing a meal. I willingly took over all the cooking in exchange for washing up and digging snow for brews.

After three long days the weather cleared somewhat. The others should be either retreating or just possibly going for the top. Either way they had been gone for seven days and we were worried. Next day should see them down one way or the other. But there was no sign of them and that evening Michael and I, who had both been avoiding the subject, discussed what to do. He suggested we made an ascent of Junction Peak, the ill-defined top that gave views across to the summit pyramid. I thought that if a rescue was needed it would take more than two of us to get even one survivor down. I found it hard to imagine that all four could be dead, unless a snowcave had collapsed or they had suffocated themselves. In either case we would be unlikely to see anything. We agreed to give it one more day and compromised by deciding to go at least up the South-West Rib the following morning with the movie camera in the hope of welcoming them down.

We left at first light and initially made fast progress up the Koksel Basin and on to the lower slopes of the broad snowy Rib. We could kick steps in the névé and on one slightly awkward ascending traverse I could see that Michael in his prime must have been a very fine climber. Eventually the sun softened the snow to the point where there was no reason to continue. We were about 500 metres above Advance Base on a brilliantly fine day. Through binoculars we took it in turns to scan the ridge high above us. There was no sign. All day we sat sweltering in the sun becoming more and more parched. The liquid we had brought up to greet the others was drunk as the chances of them descending grew slimmer and slimmer. At three in the afternoon we decided to go down but lingered until three thirty, then four. By now desperately worried, we set off down.

After losing about a hundred metres Michael stopped for one last look through the binoculars. 'I can see them,' he announced quietly but with intense emotion. I realised how worried he must have been and for a moment both of us were very near to tears of relief. After a lot of searching I could just distinguish four tiny spots against a snow patch that almost immediately vanished as they moved on to more broken ground. We sat and waited for what seemed like hours until the dots reappeared, larger now at the top of the Rib. Soon we had no need of binoculars and the dots became figures with arms and legs. Once again Michael set out to meet them. Once again I set the camera up to record the news. Once again the four approached giving absolutely no sign of success or failure. In the evening light, with superb backlit surroundings, I filmed the four as they approached and passed me, striding through knee-deep snow but looking all in. 'We've done it,' croaked Chris.

They collapsed in the snow and I realised that we had just finished all the precious fluid we had brought up for them. They were a sorry sight, with sunken cheeks, burned noses and lips and tendrils of frozen snot hanging from their noses and beards. They also smelled horrible. Briefly they told what was to become an epic story, which was that they had been marooned in 'snow coffins' – one-man slots just under the surface of the snow which was too shallow for proper snow holes – for three long stormbound days and nights before facing a protracted battle with the upper buttress which had given climbing as hard as the North Face of the Matterhorn. They had got to the top late and made a more commodious snow hole just below the summit. The next morning Chris had returned to the top to take photographs and had an unwelcome surprise. Another summit some half-mile away, which the night before had seemed lower, now looked higher. After some soul-searching they had decided they must walk across the easy ground to check it out. It had taken most of the day to find out that they were wrong and that the first peak was indeed the top. That afternoon they had only managed to descend as far as the original snow cave at the other end of the knife-edge ridge (which explained why Michael's and my calculations were a day out). Pete had had a very narrow squeak, dislodging a large rock on to his head while abseiling, and was lucky to be alive.

Just for once Michael and I travelled faster than the Gang of Four and we forged a trail down the spur and back across to Advance Base, where we lit every available stove and made brew after brew for the weary climbers. It amused me that Pete, Joe and Al, after their first mug, all cadged cigarettes off me – they had all given up before the expedition.

Joe, when he could speak properly, told me he had shot all the autoload film which meant that we had twelve minutes of film of the upper section of the mountain, including, Joe said, a dramatic summit sequence. If it had all been exposed correctly, I realised with excitement, we could have a really good film on our hands.

I spent hours cooking up every last bit of food and producing a gigantic stew, heavily spiced and smelling delicious. When everyone else had been served, Michael, who was dishing it out, spilt mine all over the tent. 'Never mind,' said Chris consolingly to Michael, 'it doesn't matter.' Not to you it doesn't, I thought less than charitably as I received a spoonful or so of cold mess scraped off the groundsheet.

Pete slept in my tent that night. He was still very hyped up over the ascent and his accident and we talked far into the night. At last he sank into exhausted sleep and silence reigned, broken only by Chris's famous snoring which kept me awake until, in another tent, Al and Joe started as well. Pete joined in, presumably out of solidarity. The nocturnal quartet reduced me first to fury then hysterical laughter. Eventually I slept.

Our arrival at Base Camp the following day coincided with the arrival of a couple of camels carrying, amongst others things, a supply of Chinese lager called, almost unbelievably, Sinkian Peeweesee and a crate of Moët et Chandon supplied by Jardine's to toast our hoped-for success. Only one bottle had broken on its strange journey across China, the rest were quickly broached and at an altitude of almost 5000 metres champagne corks hit the roof of the Base Camp tents with the force of bullets. Doctors, climbers and our Chinese helpers celebrated together, the first of many similar parties that marked our progress back to Beijing, and culminated in a banquet in the Great Hall of the People on Tiananmen Square which seemed quite over the top until we found out that we were paying for it!

Since the Kongur expedition David Wilson has gone on to much higher things, not in climbing, but in the diplomatic service. As Governor of Hong Kong he has the unenviable task of steering the troubled colony towards the day in 1997 when it reverts to Chinese sovereignty. The appointment will have given him the most profound satisfaction and fulfilment, as all his years of experience and knowledge of China have been recognised. But it has also put this most self-effacing and charming of men into the spotlight of world media, which must be a huge and constant strain. My very best memories on Kongur are of the little foray up the Pimple. Now every time I see David on television I remember sitting on that snowy summit, gazing out at that great empty panorama of Central Asia. I hope during all the turmoil and stress of his job David can sometimes look back to those precious days: then at least life was quite simple.

10

ON THE ROCKS

THE KONGUR expedition was a watershed. No sooner was I back in my Bristol flat with all the film processed and viewed, than my life started to fall apart. The death of my mother, which I had registered but not had time to come to terms with before Kongur, combined with the break-up of my second marriage, provoked an intense misery and loneliness, and just before our celebratory visit to Downing Street, a bitter blow fell on the close-knit climbing world. Al Harris was dead, killed in a head-on drunken car crash. With his death came the end of an era and I felt, with many others, that a bit of my youth had died as well. Al Rouse and I drove from our evening in Downing Street to North Wales. In the Padarn Lake, after the funeral, Harris's own sound system belted out the old Rolling Stones numbers for the last time, as we got tearfully drunk. It didn't help my mental state at all.

Throughout the black months that followed, Al and his girlfriend Hilary in Sheffield provided much-needed friendship, as I worked on the Kongur film with Chris Lister at Chameleon Films in Leeds. The film itself progressed well. The main problem was its length. At forty-five minutes it seemed about right but needed to be fifty-two to be shown on the hour slot on ITV. Eventually, in order to get screened, it was drastically cut to twenty-six minutes, a move that I bitterly resented at the time but one that in retrospect I now see was a good thing, as it preserves all the best footage and moves at a cracking pace. Joe's film at the end provided the icing on the cake and it remains the most stunning piece of film I have ever seen, shot at an altitude of over 7500 metres.

With the film finished I returned to college and went on a field trip with the students to Pembroke. One evening I switched on the car radio to listen to the news. Pete and Joe were dead on Everest. Stunned, I remembered how Michael Ward and I had watched and waited for so long the year before on Kongur. But this time they

My climbing partner, Mike Richardson.

hadn't returned. In an awful way the news had an element of in-evitability about it. I felt that their determination on Kongur was verging on the ruthless. On their own on the upper reaches of the North-East Ridge of Everest, without Chris or Al to call a halt, I could quite easily imagine them pushing too hard and for too long. Indeed Al and I had visualised exactly such a scenario months earlier. As with K2 in 1978, I had been desperately disappointed not to go to Everest. But both had ended in disaster. Deep down I wondered how I could ever justify going on another big expedition.

As I gradually recovered I decided that if there was one thing I could do to make my life better, it would be to buy a house in Sheffield. My mother had left me enough money for a deposit and after some searching I found a stone-fronted terraced house in a delightful little road in Nether Edge, a suburb of Sheffield much favoured by climbers. Paul Nunn lived just up the road. Al was to move just down the road and Laraine, who was now with another old climbing friend, Mike Richardson, was not far away. In Bristol I rented a room off Caroline White, a fellow lecturer and well-known artist and long-suffering confidante. She and I have actually lived together in various flats and houses in Bristol for longer than both my marriages put together, which says a lot for platonic relationships. Both of us appear to listen sympathetically to each other's accounts of our ups and downs, biting our lips until it is our turn to retaliate. We both admit that neither of us is actually remotely interested in what the other is talking about but use the time to think up what to say next. To an outsider, our long conversations must seem extraordinarily disjointed.

As well as moving to Sheffield, I rediscovered rock climbing. Since the Trango Tower expedition I had allowed it to slip gradually into second place. True, I still went out to Derbyshire or Wales most weekends but the social scene in the Moon and the Padarn Lake was more important than the climbs. Expeditions and films tended to take up so much time and effort that the very reason for getting involved in them in the first place was in danger of being lost. So I was well overdue for a renaissance. It came in the form of a series of apparently random chances to climb on some of Britain's most desirable but inaccessible island sea-cliffs and stacks.

Brought up on those middle-class bastions of children's literature, Enid Blyton, Arthur Ransome and Robert Louis Stevenson, I have always been fascinated by small islands. The books themselves are probably all banned now for being racist, sexist and elitist, but in their own way they fuelled a curiosity and a romantic yearning to go and explore secret coves and caves, dig for treasure, see old shipwrecks and be marooned by storms.

Lundy, in the Bristol Channel, fulfils all these criteria, yet it was not until my late thirties that I got around to going there. The treasure of course was not gold. Lundy has some of the best and most concentrated array of granite sea-cliffs in the West Country, rivalling West Penwith in their variety and seriousness. It is not an easy island to get to. Climbers are severely rationed, which is probably a good thing. Only the dedicated few get it together to go, and the cliffs are therefore never crowded. Ornithology and scuba diving are the other main recreations and, on the whole, the three activities are carried out more or less compatibly, given that Lundy is only about five kilometres long and 400 metres wide.

My first visit was with a motley team based around the Nottingham

Climbing Club, including Howard Lancashire, Pete Thexton, John English, Ron Prior and an old friend, Pip Hopkinson, who on occasion is as large as I am and is almost always more noisy. We were there to provide the light entertainment. Pete was a Lundy devotee dating back to childhood family holidays and this was his fifteenth visit. He was responsible for many new routes on the island, and was an ideal companion to have on a first excursion, when it is quite difficult to get a good idea of the many descents to the cliffs. These are often invisible from above and totally inaccessible from below without a boat. The exception is the famous Devil's Slide – a 120-metre sweep of featureless slab – the first climb to be done on Lundy.

We travelled in the old-fashioned way: on the *Polar Bear*, a converted ice-breaker that sailed from Ilfracombe to Lundy until its unfortunate demise not long after, when it ran aground on Cardiff beach. It felt a bit like a miniature *Titanic*, with ancient brass fittings and heavy mahogany furniture. As a precaution against seasickness, to which I am prone, I spent most of the voyage in the bar. We dropped anchor at Landing Craft Bay in the late afternoon and a motorboat duly came out to collect us. A tractor and trailer carried our heavy rucksacks up the rough track that led to all the various accommodation sites on the island. Unencumbered, we sauntered up behind it, childishly excited at the prospects in store for us during the coming week.

For Pip and me the visit was free of any obligation to do anything other than enjoy ourselves. Our combined age, girth and low cunning have, over the years, enabled us to develop a knack of sniffing out good but not too difficult routes on crags that maintain the illusion that we are still young rock athletes. I am still convinced that a Ron Fawcett-like physique is lying dormant, only awaiting the perfect climb to burst forth like a butterfly from the chrysalis. The reality is of course rather different and summed up by Mo, who saw me for the first time about two months after I had returned, comparatively sylphlike, from Everest. 'I see you've become the self of your former shadow,' he greeted me.

On Lundy we didn't have to look far for climbs that flattered to deceive. Several, like the Devil's Slide itself, are minor classics and one is an absolutely brilliant little climb. It is called Diamond Solitaire and, though only graded Very Severe 4c, it has an atmosphere that one normally would only expect to find on a much larger cliff.

On a gloriously fine morning Pip and I walked across the short, springy turf to the ruins of the Old Battery, where rusty cannons are evidence of a romantic past. An easy scramble down and a short traverse brought the appropriately named Flying Buttress into view. I was amazed and impressed. A huge, leaning slab was propped crazily against the cliff. A great arch underneath seemed to forbid access, but at low tide we could boulder-hop across a deep channel to a damp, dark chimney. This led easily to a foot ledge below the sweeping slab and the main difficulties. Leading today, I paused and weighed up the main problem. On my left was a thin crack in which I placed enough small nuts to moor a battleship. Then I took some of them out as they had covered all the best handholds. The footholds, however, were away on the right, and the main problem was to persuade myself that I was not about to do two different climbs at the same time. Hands would explore one way and feet the other.

At last I sorted out what to do and immediately fell victim to the Great Slab Inertia Syndrome. This all-too-common occurrence ensures that however much one wants to move up, one is abruptly foiled, apparently by a superior intelligence than the brain, which stops arms and legs moving at the last possible instant. Several attempts led to no more than the merest twitch of the leg muscles but no upward progress at all. To the non-climber, the phenomenon is best likened to a learner driver stalling on a hill start. Phase two of the syndrome involves, in my case, rapid gulping, a dry mouth and occasionally leaning my forehead against the rock and shutting my eyes.

Relief came suddenly. For no particular reason I moved up, and up again. I realised that there was a big, usable hold on the left of the crack and pulled, then stood on it. 'Piece of piss actually,' I shouted down to Pip in the time-honoured way. I climbed another few metres and, impressed with my courage, skill and commitment, belayed before I could get frightened again. Pip climbed quickly up and we changed belays. A friend, Chris Griffiths (known to all as Bladder), who was a very keen photographer, arrived at the foot of the descent route just as I set out on the upper slab and took some stunning photographs. The climbing was much easier, falling into the 'you show me big holds and I'll show you good technique' variety. Posed above the great arch with only the air and green sea below it was possible to indulge in a little cautious showing off. Sixty feet of intoxicating movement led to easy ground and a final storming of the Old Battery. Lacking only a cutlass in my mouth and a brace of pistols tucked into my harness I vaulted nimbl(ish)ly over the crumbling wall and brought Pip up, laughing at the ease of the climbing and the cheek of the position.

The last time I went to Lundy I repeated the route with Bob Toogood. Bob led the whole climb in about five minutes then dissolved laughing as I gibbered on a tight rope, totally unable to second what I had previously led. At last I found the right sequence and suddenly completed the hard bit.

'Much easier this time,' I said before I could stop myself.

Bob was incredulous. 'How can you possibly say that? I've just pulled you up it! Curran, you're a complete fraud!'

Lundy is only one of the many islands around Britain that have superb climbing on them. Perhaps the least likely were the Channel Islands. Jersey is famous for sun, sea, beaches, duty free booze, *Bergerac* and tax avoidance, but not rock climbing. Then Ian Smith, a friend and well-known still photographer living in Sheffield, persuaded a group of us to go over at Easter to have a look. The parents of a friend of his, Bill Dark, had moved to Jersey and Bill waxed eloquent over the many climbing possibilities on the island. In 1976 a climbing magazine had published an account of a few easy climbs done in the sixties and seventies, but the information was all vague and unconvincing.

Rucksacks, handbags, suitcases, holdalls, thirteen in total, lay scattered around the Weymouth quayside. Enough for a medium-sized Himalayan expedition, but only the bare essentials for us. Close inspection would have revealed suntan oil, baby lotion, assorted beach wear, no less than sixty-five pairs of knickers and, almost as an afterthought, some climbing gear and a few ropes. In addition to the climbing team, which was Al Rouse, Phil Burke, Richard Haszko, Ian, Bill and me, there were also Viv (Ian's wife), Hilary (Al's girlfriend), Cass (my girlfriend) and Gemma and Becky, who were responsible for most of the underwear. Inspired by one of Al's more ingenious wheezes, I had been persuaded to buy a British Rail family railcard which enabled us to travel at vastly reduced cost from Sheffield to Jersey. Al said that he and Phil could count as my offspring, as well as my two girls, ignoring the fact that this would have made me a father at the age of seven or eight (Phil was slightly evasive about his real age).

Quids in, and not apparently required to show our family trees or birth certificates, we set forth on the high seas. Eight hours and God alone knows how many gin and tonics later we were poured ashore at St Helier, well on the way to having redressed the balance of the savings we had made with the railcard. I wondered what Bill would think at the arrival of what appeared to be a group of survivors of an explosion in a gin distillery. But he was very understanding. In the same state as us in fact. It was a good sign.

We had been told that the cliffs were sound granite up to around the twenty-metre mark, but above that they degenerated into rotten rock. It is not hard to imagine our delight the next morning when we took our first walk around the north-west coast and discovered what appeared to be another Cornwall. True it was a bit smaller and the crags not quite so extensive, but it was as if we had been transported back to Bosigran or Chair Ladder in the 1930s. All the classic lines were waiting to be done (as of course were the hard ones). The rock appeared to be perfectly sound orange and grey granite.

Being firmly of 'B' team status, I joined Bill and Ian for a look at a crag called Le Vyi, a small, immaculately solid crag opposite a large pointed rock, vaguely reminiscent of Porthmiona Island at Bosigran. In my hung-over state it took me a few minutes to realise that I had been manoeuvred into the lead. Watching Bill solo happily across a steep, slippery wall to belay beneath a fine corner crack, I was mystified and slightly flattered at his faith in my ability. An hour later and fifteen metres higher, Ian decided that photographing the 'A' team was a better bet. Richard, when told of my rate of progress, commented, 'I've seen continents drift faster!'

To my delight I eventually climbed the steep, thin and quite fingery corner. In deference to the aforementioned TV series, I called it Bergercrack. Its original grade, Hard Very Severe 5a, has been retained in the new guidebook to the area. It is also described as 'worthy of special mention', though this could of course be merely due to the fact that I managed to get up it.

The climb was just a pipe-opener in a brilliant week. The climbing was magnificent, the weather perfect, the company wonderful, the bullshitting outrageous, and the booze was ridiculously cheap. The girls turned the colour of old violins instantly and all of us, bar Al Rouse, spent our time alternating between beach, bar and buttress. Al, who like me had found a great rekindling of rock-climbing enthusiasm after his years of extreme alpine and Himalayan performance, was committed to climbing in a way that made St Paul's conversion on the road to Damascus seem about as convincing as Margaret Thatcher's belief in socialism.

Fired with the zeal of an ayatollah, Al spent every waking moment plotting and scheming his next new route. Phil and Richard took it in turns to climb with him, nicknaming him 'Moriarty' as he devised ever more fiendish plots to drag us away from the beach. On the spectacular wall of Le Pinnacle de l'Etacq, he and Phil produced the

Bill Dark and, above him, the author in Jersey on the first ascent of Bergercrack.

Jersey masterpiece Tax Exile at E5 6a 5b. With Richard he did Steel City, E2 5c, and the great and surprisingly easy Perihelion at Hard VS 5a on the imposing left wall of La Tête d'Ane. Richard surprised himself by leading me up the right wall of the same cliff. Senior Citizens is only HVS 4c but once again a classic jug-pulling exercise on big holds. Then Al, still thirsty for new routes, went to Le Vyi where I had spotted a fine, steep edge on the right of Bergercrack. It looked far too hard for me (and was) but Al, climbing at his brilliant best, cruised the thin pitch to produce Citizens' Edge at E2 5c. I followed on a predictably tight rope and Richard, who had not enjoyed the steep descent, was made to savour every move to the full as Al gave him a very slack rope all the way up.

In all we produced twenty-one new routes and put Jersey firmly on the rock-climbing map. But I remember it best as a brief interlude of sheer fun, for Al's company and enthusiasm on what was his last happy and trouble-free climbing holiday. After that a series of personal problems and expeditions that either failed or were fraught with tensions led Al down the path that ended on K2 in 1986.

It was a time when the girls were still children and yet becoming old enough for me to enjoy their company as friends. And with Cass I had a brilliant relationship. Tall, blonde and outrageously outspoken, Cass is a one-off. She is a Bristol teacher, devoted to her job but at the same time determined to enjoy every minute of her full and varied life. It says a lot for her that she managed to cope with my lifestyle for over four years before she reluctantly accepted that I was a non-starter for a more permanent relationship, as my undistinguished marital track record proved.

Another great sea-cliff climbing area is Pembroke, which had a major new route boom in the late seventies. More by luck than good judgment I was involved in some of the early plunderings and was even responsible for a few easy routes of my own. The most memorable visit was Easter 1980. The whole climbing world, it seemed, was stirred by bush telegraphy to assemble at Bosherston Farm campsite and, as Rab Carrington said, 'Anything less than three new routes a day doesn't count!'

A star-studded collection of names like Pat Littlejohn, Brian Hall, John Porter, Dave Cook, Ken Wilson and Ben and Marion Wintringham produced over seventy routes in a week.

Also present from America was the one and only Henry Barber. 'Hot' Henry had been at the BMC conference in Buxton and then spent a week with me and Laraine. As *Crags* magazine had bestowed the 'worst climber in the world' title on me I was amused to climb with one of the best. Henry and I went into Derbyshire every day and he led classic after classic. He often climbed barefoot to give me a chance. On Wee Doris at Stoney Middleton he actually found the top few moves awkward. At the top he burst into a manic peal of laughter. 'There y'are, Jim – even the best of us can shake, rattle and roll, just like you!' A week with Henry was a week in the fast lane climbing, boozing and living at speed. I drove him from Pembroke to Bristol to catch a train to Heathrow. 'Hey – one last climb?' We rushed up Bonington's classic Malbogies and raced to the station, where I didn't see him again for nine years, by which time a lot had changed.

11

WHAT TOOK YOU SO LONG?

IN JANUARY 1983 I endured my fortieth birthday. With no projects on the horizon I was desperate for an expedition or film. Then, during a fund-raising disco in Bristol, I was approached, half-jokingly, and asked whether I would do a climb for charity. Well on the way to alcoholic euphoria, I replied, 'One? Why only one? We'll do a hundred!'

The question was addressed to me by the wife of my head of department at Bristol. Sheila Murison was involved in Radio Lollipop, a radio station and charitable organisation for children in hospital. Having seen my own children in hospitals in Bristol, Sheffield and Manchester, I felt it was a more than worthy cause to support.

With me at the disco was Phil Kershaw, a mature student studying Fine Art at Bristol, and a good climber with whom I had already done a few of the classic climbs in the Avon Gorge. Together we evolved a plan to do a hundred climbs from the north of Scotland to Land's End, taking in Ben Nevis, Scafell and Snowdon, as well as climbs in Derbyshire, Pembroke and the south-west. We would visit all the best climbing areas of Britain and complete the journey in ten days. To start with, but not actually included in either the hundred climbs or the ten days, we would climb the Old Man of Hoy. This was a long-standing ambition. Like most climbers I had been captivated by the original BBC Outside Broadcast in the 1960s, but for many years felt it would be beyond me. Then when I realised I could probably do it (given a determined leader who was strong enough to give me a tight rope all the way), the opportunity never seemed to arise. It is a long way to the Orkneys and it isn't cheap either. But here was a golden opportunity to knock it off in a good cause.

Paul Nunn, doyen of Peak District and Karakoram climbing.

We didn't really know whether what we were planning was realistic or wildly optimistic. We aimed to keep the standard at an average of Very Severe, and I hoped that wherever possible we could pick off classics that we hadn't done before. All through the summer term we tried to climb as much as possible; I gave up drinking for a bet from Easter until the end of term and Phil gave up smoking. A car hire firm in Bristol lent us a van and the local radio station agreed to cover our progress with phone-ins every night as a way of generating sponsorship. Everything seemed to be falling into place. Sheila's husband, my boss Neil, decided to come with us to share the driving which promised to be as tiring as the climbing. Neil is a talented artist, so he would cover the trip with a series of watercolours and we would have an exhibition of these and our photographs to round the whole thing off. Suddenly I started getting nervous. It all seemed to be getting very complex and we didn't have much leeway in the very likely event of bad weather.

The day after the term ended we drove leisurely up to Sheffield. Paul Nunn was to come with us to Hoy to lend his caving ropes for abseiling on and, best of all, his company. Paul had never been to Hoy either, though he had explored several other sea stacks in the company of Tom Patey in the mid-sixties, and had been with Patey when he was killed abseiling on The Maiden, a small sea stack off the Sutherland coast. Since then Paul had not climbed a sea stack. Perhaps doing the Old Man of Hoy would help expunge the memories.

The Pentland Firth is normally rough, but on this occasion it was an almost flat calm, misty with a hazy sun trying to break through. In no danger of parting with our good Scottish breakfasts, we lounged on the deck of the *St Ola*, occasionally peering ahead to catch the first glimpse of the Orkney Islands. At last the horizon blurred and darkened and the southern coast of Hoy came into view. We knew the *St Ola* sailed past the Old Man itself but for a long time all we could see was an almost unbroken line of sandstone cliffs. An Orcadian guessed what we were looking for. 'It's just behind Rora Head. You won't have to wait long.'

Slowly, as we came abreast of the headland, the Old Man of Hoy revealed itself reflected in an oily, still sea. But behind again was the huge rampart of St John's Head – 340 metres of rusty red sandstone. The Old Man was well named, a wrinkled, tottering and somewhat fragile structure that seemed quite diminutive against its huge back-drop. There was even something slightly humorous in its appearance and I remembered reading somewhere that from certain angles it looked like an elderly Victorian gentleman in a top hat. Somehow it was a lot less daunting than I had expected and I felt certain we would romp up it the following day.

Stromness is on the mainland of Orkney. On our extremely brief visit I felt it had the same sort of charm as a Cornish fishing village must have had at the turn of the century with its narrow cobbled streets and air of tranquillity once the *St Ola* had departed.

In the afternoon we boarded the motorboat and crossed the short Hoy Sound, passing a wrecked merchant ship, reminder of the First World War when boats were scuttled by the navy to prevent German submarines from entering Scapa Flow and decimating the British fleet that used the huge, natural harbour for shelter. Cormorants lined every deck and railing, gazing at us with cold and beady eyes and ruffling their oily feathers. It was like a scene from the classic Hitchcock film, *The Birds*.

We landed on Hoy and ordered a (or possibly *the*) taxi to drive us to Rackwick Bay where we could camp. In glorious, golden, early evening light we trundled westwards down the single-track road past Ward Hill, the highest point in the Orkneys, on one side and the Knap of Treviglen on the other. Framed in the middle was the blue sea and short cropped grass of Rackwick Bay. On either side were red, crumbling cliffs about a hundred metres high. We pitched our two small tents outside a derelict bothy. Alongside were camped the Stromness Boys' Brigade in big old-fashioned bell tents. They were, I thought, survivors of a bygone age, polite and well-behaved with a quality of innocence that few, if any, inner-city kids could ever possess. In this idyllic setting I felt a wave of nostalgia that a way of life was still just surviving up here but might not much longer. Something in these children made me very aware of what had been lost in the rat race of what we fondly believe is the real world.

After a meal we decided to carry all the climbing gear over to the top of the cliff opposite the Old Man, to save ourselves the trouble of doing it early next morning, and to have a close-up look at our objective. On a warm, muggy evening, with the orange sun still well above the horizon at ten p.m., we strolled casually along the narrow path up and over the cliffs leading across a streak of bleak moorland. In the distance a small tower protruded, the last few feet of the Old Man. Suddenly there was a squawk, a rush of wind, and a dark shape swooped low. It was a skua, and it obviously didn't like us. Skuas, known as 'bonxies' in the Hebrides and Orkneys, are large brown solitary birds that pursue other gulls, forcing them to disgorge their food. Occasionally they kill them. Skuas are unpleasant creatures, and on this occasion we had walked too near its nest. Irate and aggressive, like a feathered Messerschmidt 109, it came for us out of the sun with guttural cries, swooping just over our heads. The Orcadian farmers apparently put pieces of slate in their flat hats to stop skuas' beaks or talons cracking skulls, which they are easily capable of.

I found the attack distinctly unnerving and by the time we reached the top of the cliff opposite the Old Man I was far more apprehensive than I had been two hours earlier. Approaching the edge Neil, a non-climber with no head for heights, was reduced to crawling. Pride just stopped me joining him as Paul, Phil and I stood and stared across and down the awesome drop.

In the late evening light the Old Man of Hoy was revealed in all his majesty. One hundred and forty metres of slender stratified sandstone, dark against the setting sun and surrounded by wheeling, diving sea-birds whose mournful cries echoed back and forth in the still evening air. Having dropped the climbing gear off at the top of the descent path, we walked back to the sanctuary of Rackwick

Bay rather more pensively than we had set out.

We wanted to get climbing by seven a.m., and be back by early afternoon, for the taxi was returning to pick us up. I had brought a Sony Walkman and microphone to record the events of the next ten days in order, I hoped, to make a short programme for Radio Lollipop. 'Now here we are at the top of a cliff in the Orkney Islands and you can hear all around the wail of the sea-birds. In a minute a big brown one, called a skua, will try to attack me and I will try to record its – fuck off, you little bastard!' Once again the skua whistled over my head. Hastily I turned the tape-recorder off and scuttled away after the others.

Half an hour later we gathered at the foot of the climb. Unlike the Old Man of Stoer or Am Buchaille, the Old Man of Hoy is not, strictly speaking, a sea stack at all for it stands on a granite plinth and is connected to the mainland by a causeway of boulders that were once a natural arch. With no danger of drowning it is at least possible to start the route in a composed frame of mind. Just.

I had prudently tied on to the end of every rope I could see which meant I would be in the middle of a rope of three, which suited me admirably. Phil and Paul quibbled about who was to lead what, for they both wanted the prize second pitch, the hard one. Phil, who had psyched himself up for it, got it in exchange for Paul leading all the rest. Paul set off with a great clanking of gear and climbed in his inimitable style, massively confident, economical and unfussy up easy but very suspect rock to belay about thirty metres up. I joined him, nerves almost squeaking in anticipation of what was about to happen.

The rock was dusty, friable and offputting. It was important to distribute your weight evenly and avoid snatching at big holds: in other words, to climb well.

Phil joined us and, leaning out on the belays, he and Paul peered round the corner at the main obstacle. This was the famous overhanging crack. A traverse over a big drop led to the first overhang, split by a hand jam crack. Despite his obvious apprehension, Phil made quick, decisive progress up through the first overhang and carried on slowly but steadily up the remainder of the pitch, which was out of sight. All too soon it was time for me to unclip, swallow hard and set off across the traverse, first stepping down to a narrow foot ledge then moving with increasing confidence as the ropes above ran nearer and nearer to the vertical with each step, and the possibility of a big pendulum grew less.

The first overhang was easy and for a few feet above it I felt quite in control, until I looked up at the widening crack, turning almost into a chimney which reared over my head. It looked appalling. I concentrated on one move at a time until I found myself wedged uncomfortably in the depths of the crack wondering what to do next. An ancient sling hung from an equally antique wooden wedge. Knowing that farting about here wouldn't do me any good, I grabbed the sling, hauled mightily and with a scrabbling-thrutching-bridging kind of movement, found myself tantalisingly close to getting round the second overhang. 'For Christ's sake, take in. Take in tight!' In addition to the ordinary backrope to Paul, I was trailing a doubled non-stretch caving rope to leave in place for the diagonal abseil back to the first stance. Without this safety rope you would simply abseil into space, for the pitch overhangs by five metres. But now, fighting the overhang, the weight and drag of these ropes was beginning to tell. This was combined with my own bulk and when at last I heaved up and into a bridging position above the roof I was quite shattered. The corner was just too wide for easy jams and too rounded to layback. There was about ten metres more of quite sustained and technical bridging before I pulled, or was pulled, on to big friendly holds to find a grinning Phil tied to an enormous natural thread belay around which were draped countless ageing slings and bits of rope. 'Enjoyed that, did you?'

My arms were so pumped I couldn't pull the ropes, so Phil brought Paul up while I took photographs looking straight down the corner past Paul to the sea far below. Paul stormed up the pitch and arrived on the stance. His white T-shirt was covered in red sand with a liberal patina of fulmar excrement and vomit mixed in. He smelled like a sardine canning factory. 'Seems like a rather dirty old man to me,' he muttered as he took Phil's gear and set off up the middle pitches.

These were much easier – short, steep walls set back from each other by narrow ledges on which dozens of fulmars sat, eyeing us curiously, obviously weighing up whether or not our presence justified a well-aimed stream of vomit. On one belay I stood looking out at an almost psychedelic landscape – red sandstone, covered in patches of green and yellow lichen, blue sky, green sea with white foam tossing around the base of the stack and the air full of birds, plunging and swooping around. Tendrils of seagull shit constantly fell past into space. It was a technicolour riot of reeling perspectives and outrageous rock formations. The Old Man's horizontal strata had endless variations caused by rain and wind. Worn crenellations and gargoyles of weathered sandstone twisted and thrust their peculiar forms into space. It was a mystery how, from a distance, such apparently random forms could take on the illusion of regular architecture. Quickly we reached the final stance. Above us was a vertical corner of much sounder rock, covered in holds and giving a steep, sensational finish to the climb. Bombproof protection and classic hand jams in the corner and on the horizontal breaks made this possibly the most enjoyable pitch of all.

Exultant, we all gathered on the summit, which despite its size gives an illusion of security and I felt quite comfortable standing up and shuffling about. The smoke from my cigarette drifted straight up. Opposite on the cliff top Neil had been painting diligently, despite the attentions of midges and horse flies. He was now taking photographs with my Canon F1. We waved across to him and I did a bit of punching the air in the style of a professional footballer, but this made me look and feel rather foolish and insecure, so I sat down while Paul rigged the abseils. It was eleven a.m.

It was only an hour later when we all got down. The abseiling, which I had been dreading, was fast and efficient, with absolutely idiot-proof anchor points. (I noticed however that in the excitement and suppressed tension Phil's Oldham accent got noticeably broader as the day progressed.) The big pitch was predictably a trouser-filler. As I stepped carefully down the corner I was suddenly aware of a huge void with the two caving ropes curving away to the stance below. The feeling of jumping out of an aircraft and into space was quite overwhelming.

As I spun down Paul pulled the ropes in and I swung clumsily into the belay ledge. 'Holy shit!' I croaked with relief through a dry mouth. At that moment, having escaped all the attentions of the fulmars, a gigantic gobbet of oily bird dropping hit me on the back of my neck and spattered my still pristine T-shirt.

By one p.m. we had regained the cliff top and Neil, who was as euphoric as ourselves. Plenty of time to stroll back, take down the tents and wait for the taxi.

By four we were back at the landing stage and by five we were unexpectedly on the *St Ola*, which had made an unscheduled return voyage to Stromness. At seven thirty, bemused and still high on the adrenalin buzz of the climb, we were ordering steaks in a Thurso hotel. It had happened almost too quickly. What's more, we had gained an unexpected day, which threw our schedule into confusion for I had assumed that we would waste the whole of the next day on the return from the Orkneys. Paul, who would be going back to Sheffield from Inverness the following evening, suggested a solution: to drive round to Sheigra on the north-west coast south of Cape Wrath, where it just so happened there was a new route crying out to be done . . . We could still get down to drop Paul off on the sleeper tomorrow evening and press on to Fort William for the night.

Still giggling to ourselves at the events of the day, we set off, driving westwards into the setting sun across the very top of Scotland. We passed the surreal and sinister spheres of Dounreay Nuclear Research Station, with a shudder at their strange, intrusive presence on such a bleak and unspoiled landscape, and drove on, with distant views of Ben Loyal and Ben Hope, blue and alluring in the evening light. We were entering what I always thought of as Paul's spiritual home. For over twenty years he has been the driving force in bringing Sheffield teams up to the north-west every Whitsun and grabbing dozens of new routes on the extensive sea cliffs of Cape Wrath and inland crags of Foinavon and Arkle. I had never got beyond Gairloch and one awful visit to Carnmore Crag with Steve Durkin, about which the least said the better. I was fascinated to get to see what for me had become a slightly mysterious area.

Another night in a layby then a short drive through the fishing port of Kinlochbervie and on to the sand dunes and green cropped grass of Sheigra. A beautiful unspoilt beach and any number of tiny crags but no sign of a decent new route. 'Don't worry, it's not far.' Paul set off up the steep hillside behind the beach and, sure enough, on the other side of the headland was an immaculate crag of black gneiss. Several routes had already been done by the marauding hordes from south Yorkshire. Phil and I did an easy warm-up route and Paul inspected his line, a blank and intimidating arête with side runners in an adjoining groove. I'm afraid, still aching from my fight on the Old Man of Hoy, I relegated myself to photographer for this one, and Phil, who followed, confirmed its difficulty – about E2 5c. As it was done for Radio Lollipop, Paul named it the Big Lick (but we tactfully called it Lollipop).

We left for Inverness, dropped Paul off with regret, and carried on down the Great Glen, arriving at Fort William at midnight. At the same time about five million midges arrived and I spent the humid night wrapped up in the tent while Neil and Phil suffered in the van.

Another dawn start (to avoid further punishment as much as anything else) and Phil and I walked up the Allt a' Mhuilinn towards the North-East Buttress of Ben Nevis. It was my first return visit since filming *The Bat*. This time the weather was perfect, despite the presence of several large snow-fields lingering into July after a hard winter.

As the ascent of the Ben was on our list of prescribed summits we chose a route to get us to the top as efficiently as possible. Minus One Direct was reputed to be good. Wearing only T-shirt and shorts I had an ignominious slither up, over and into a small bergschrund at the foot of the buttress before I managed to touch rock. Phil was feeling strong and did most of the leading.

After about 200 metres of sustained VS climbing I realised that Ben Nevis in summer was much the same as in winter: far bigger and longer than it is given credit for. We gained the crest of the North-East Buttress itself and unroped, soloing interminably on easy rocks until we reached the infamous Man Trap. I had been here before with Paul in winter and had been impressed with its difficulty. Now warm and dry, the short, grey granite wall, scoured and polished by hundreds of grating crampon points, seemed no easier than in winter. Shamefully, we roped up again, suffering what I considered the first signs of altitude sickness. The summit remained as far away as ever but at last, by studiously ignoring it, we surprised it, and revelled briefly in a perfect view before starting the long knee-wrecking descent to Neil, the van, endless brews and a Chinese takeaway in Fort William.

With two days of our ten used up (for Hoy didn't count) we still had ninety-eight routes to do (ninety-seven in Phil's case). Though things were going to plan, I was relieved that we had done Scotland and could get down to the Lakes to start knocking the score along a bit. The weather was perfect and seemed to be set fair for at least the next three or four days.

Shepherds Crag in Borrowdale was not a particularly imaginative venue to choose but it was small, near the road and had lots of easy climbs. A late pub lunch saw us sitting outside in the sun, seven routes to the good, waiting for our next support climber to cheer us up.

Chris Bonington arrived early. This is a sentence that has probably never been written before and is unlikely to be so again. He also supplied his own second, which meant each pair could climb alongside each other, Chris, with becoming modesty, announced that he was climbing really well, so Phil and I tagged along to Black Crag where Chris led Vertigo and we sneaked up the more amenable Shroud.

That evening Chris, who seemed genuinely keen on our strange outing, took us to the Packhorse in Keswick and reminisced about how he had once climbed White Slab on Cloggy, Central Buttress on Scafell and Centurion on the Ben in under twenty-four hours! The driving had been more frightening than the climbing on that occasion. It was one of those pub nights when pints of beer disappeared by magic. Far from helping us on our way, Chris's enthusiasm was nearly responsible for the whole trip foundering in a colossal hang-over. But this was but a taste of things to come. After three drunken philosophers had eaten their fish and chips round a litter-bin in the middle of Keswick, Neil, the fourth and only sober one, drove Phil and me to Wasdale Head.

Next morning dawned misty and grey, or perhaps it was just us. We walked grimly up to Hollowstones where the sun broke through to reveal the superb sweep of Scafell Crag. It had to be the classic Central Buttress, a route neither of us had done. We were oppressed by both tradition and trepidation as well as tremendous hangovers. By the time we reached the Great Flake it was obvious that Phil would be today's hero. He advanced decisively to the chockstone, and then equally decisively retreated. After several false starts he flung himself at the horrible overhanging layback and was up. Laybacking for the obese over-forties is a technique to be avoided whenever possible, but here there was no alternative. I remembered reading a warning in Ken Wilson's *Hard Rock* about rope mismanagement here, but couldn't remember what it was until, in mid-layback, I realised the rope was jammed behind the flake. Phil said later he had never before heard anyone scream for both tight and slack rope simultaneously. After that the rest of the route passed off without incident.

Chris had enlightened us the previous night by telling us Derbyshire- and North Wales-based ignoramuses that Scafell Pike was the highest mountain in England. This unwelcome bit of news meant that we had an extra half-hour's walk in our rock boots to tick off another obligatory ascent. We should, I suppose, have done Botterill's Slab or Mickledore Grooves but didn't and buggered off forthwith without a backward glance. Derbyshire was beckoning with the prospect of easy pickings and also baths, beds and square meals.

Stanage on a Saturday morning, at the unheard-of hour of seven thirty, was quiet and oppressive. The silence was rudely broken by the arrival of Pip Hopkinson to barrack us into climbing about thirty-five VSs on gritstone. It was hot and humid and as the first sweaty hand jams slid into the vertical cracks and clouds of chalk drifted into the air so did language deteriorate and tempers fray.

So far Phil had been the driving force but today I was climbing quite well. Phil at that time had climbed extensively in Wales and on limestone and although brought up on gritstone, seemed to have temporarily lost the knack of climbing it. I was revelling in the moves and couldn't resist rubbing the fact in. But in the heat and humidity I was finding everything irritating. Luckily Paul reappeared to ensure that we maintained our standards both of climbing and behaviour. So did 'Uncle' Nat Allen, who at the age of fifty something ran up climbs that a man half his age would be pleased with. To save time (and keep us from coming to blows) we split up, and climbing in two pairs we alternately led and seconded climbs on ropes already left in place.

We could have quite happily allowed the standards to drop but Paul and Nat insisted that they rose. Routes like Congo Corner, which I have always found hard, Ginny Come Lately and the hideous Agony Crack were all climbed instead of nice, easy-angled alternatives next to them.

The day was split with the arrival of two friends, Maria and Sarah, bringing a hamper full of cold chicken salad, garlic bread, cheese, potatoes and white wine. The latter was a mistake and Phil, who was going out with Maria at the time, seemed to be on the verge of giving up. Urgently I reminded him of our purpose in life which was to suffer. Neil and Pip had gone down to Hathersage to bring back urgent supplies of liquid. When they returned at closing time they were indeed carrying huge quantities but it was all in their stomachs. Neil added insult to injury by producing some of his best watercolours on the whole trip in front of a large, curious crowd who were far more impressed by his efforts than our own.

By now we were both flagging badly and having got to number thirty-six for the day, we stopped. This was significant for it was also Phil's birthday of the same number. In the evening a surprise birthday party with another superb feast and over-indulgence ensured we were late to bed with another gruelling day to follow.

Phil's return to the land of the living was a miserable affair. By Sunday lunchtime a wraithlike figure was propped up at the bottom of the Roaches moaning faintly. We had already done six routes. I wanted to do at least twenty. A violent thunderstorm, Maria, Sarah and Paul all arrived at much the same time, but I was not to be deflected. When the rain stopped I dragged the remains of Kershaw up route after route, reminding him that he had harboured ambitions to do climbs of the calibre of Sloth and the Mincer. No chance of that today. Eventually, scraping the very bottom of the barrel, we sneaked off to Windgather, the easiest crag in the whole of Derbyshire, to get the numbers up before Phil collapsed completely.

North Wales was the only place in Britain not bathed in sunshine. Bloody typical, I thought, as our proposed day of classic VSs on Cloggy receded into the mists. Instead, setting out from Mo and Jackie's where we had arrived late the previous evening, we toiled up Cwm Glas to Cyrn Las with its all-time classic climb, Main Wall. Despite having done it several times before, it is still one of the best outings in Wales and Phil and I climbed it with a surge of energy and enthusiasm. This faded suddenly at the top, as we toiled over to the

Parson's Nose and soloed up its rocky crest, like a miniature version of Tower Ridge on Ben Nevis. At last we reached Snowdon summit in the company of a stray dog and with visibility down to a few inches. That at least was all the uphill walking over and done with.

An hour later we were eating ice-creams and drinking cans of beer at Mo's. Jackie was preparing yet another feast but wouldn't let us eat anything more until we had gone up to the Llanberis Pass and done at least five routes.

Out into fresh air and toiling up the five-minute walk to Carreg Wastad my prayers were answered as the rain began to fall in earnest. Phil scraped up Shadow Wall and I teetered up a sodden Crackstone Rib which brought up the magic three-quarters mark. Then we called it a day. Now we had three days left to do just twenty-five more climbs. Back at Mo's I rang up Radio West in Bristol for our daily phone-in to record our progress. My attempt at a switched on sports commentary was broadcast live around Bristol but spoilt by Mo's hysterical giggles in the background and shouts of 'lying bastard'.

In what was also turning into a ten-day alcoholic marathon we left Mo's and a sober Neil drove us, both unconscious, to Pembroke. We awoke outside a garage in Pembroke village, waiting for it to open. Neil had got lost several times in the night and almost run out of diesel fuel. He looked as shattered as we felt.

We were aiming to do twelve routes which certainly meant finding crags with big holds and easy angles. This called for my exhaustive knowledge of the Pembrokeshire coastline where, over the years, soft options had become the rule rather than the exception. So far during the trip one of us (normally Phil) was always going better than the other. Our lows had fortunately never coincided and so it was today. Phil had been a tower of strength yesterday but I was enjoying the hot sun, white rock and green sea. Six routes in the morning then lunch at Bosherston and off to Bow Shaped Slab and a sudden reversal of roles. Hardly able to remember how to clip into a descendeur, let alone climb, the afternoon degenerated into a blur of misery – abseil, tie into belay, pay out rope, unbelay, climb, take out runners, don't drop them, reach top, abseil, tie on . . . Phil going like a machine. Eleven routes, one to go. Then it all seemed to change. The sun disappeared. It was cold and slightly eerie. Low tide, no wind, a grey sea and a feeling of impending danger. Phil looked at me. 'Come on, let's piss off before we have an accident.'

So we came to Bristol and the Gorge. After two weeks away doing proper climbs with real holds could we remember how to climb in the quirky Avon style? Surprisingly we could and Unknown Wall,

Gronk, Floating Voter and Jasper slipped past quickly. Then the Lich, Malbogies and Central Rib. 'Better jack it in now, Phil – there'll be bugger all left to do in Cornwall.' That was our last mistake.

In the evening my girlfriend Cass surpassed all the other meals with a sumptuous banquet. It was almost a premature celebration, for Cornwall, we thought, would be just a formality.

Neil drove the last leg and at two in the morning we bivouacked outside the Climbers Club hut at Bosigran. Predictably we were woken by the plummy tones of that rare old bird, the Upper Class Crinkly defending his nest. 'Please move your van, this is private property.'

'It's all right,' I yawned, 'I'm a member.'

'Member? What's your name?'

'Jim Curran.'

'Jim Perrin – you're not Jim Perrin!'

Eventually we were allowed into the hut for breakfast and I explained the reasons for our presence. Having done ninety-three climbs in the last nine days gave us the moral high ground and we left several brews later with wishes of good luck and a few more pounds raised for Radio Lollipop.

On the last day everything fell apart for both of us. We were shattered and my knees ached from all the descending. We did the Bosigran classics Doorpost and Little Brown Jug. Then suddenly we both seized up. Only five more routes to go. It was blazing hot and very calm. We drove round to Sennen Cove and wobbled precariously up four Severes that anywhere else would be given VS. We had to do one more before seven thirty.

Round to Land's End where we laughed at ourselves as we remembered that we had planned to finish with Yankee Doodle, a steep, strenuous jamming crack. Now we would be hard pushed to climb anything. In the end we settled for Cormorant Slab, an undistinguished Severe which Phil led almost as badly as I seconded it. I pulled over the top at seven fifteen with relief. It was done. No more climbing. Phil gave me a narrow-eyed sideways look. 'Don't tell me – you want to row the Atlantic next.'

Jubilant, we coiled the rope, looking out at a steely sky. The Longships Lighthouse and the Wolf Rock were black and sharp against a bright, calm sea. Thunder grumbled in the distance and, as we adjourned to the Land's End pub for a pint, the first heavy drops of rain began to fall.

That night we slept soundly, occasionally stirring to the crash of thunder and the steady drum of rain on the roof of the van. In the

'Don't tell me – you want to row the Atlantic next.' Phil Kershaw after we had completed our hundred climbs.

morning it was still scything down. 'Okay, chaps,' – Phil doing his best RAF impersonation – 'rest easy – no Jerry bombers today.' I turned over in my sleeping-bag and slept until lunchtime.

So we'd done it, just. It had been the best British climbing holiday either of us had ever had. What's more, we had raised some £1500 for Radio Lollipop and Neil had produced about seventy watercolours. To my amazement Ron Fawcett of all people told me later that he had been impressed with our efforts. He must have been for a couple of years later Ron soloed one hundred Extremes in Derbyshire – in a day! This put us firmly in our place, as did Joe Brown's comment when I told him proudly what we had done. His face creased into the famous, toothy grin. 'What took you so long?'

12

DON

Don WHILLANS. It's a name as dour and uncompromising as its owner was, with a hint of sharpness there as well. He was and will always be a legend: an acerbic man with a mean streak; a mountaineer of genius; a dry, humorous observer of life; on occasion a fat, beer-swilling layabout; an aggressive and brilliant rock climber in his youth; a mellow and wise adviser in his later years.

Don Whillans was all these things and much, much more. I was lucky in knowing him in what were to prove the last years of his life. I grew very fond of the rotund, powerful little man who quite regularly parked his motorbike or VW camper outside my house and announced his arrival in his normal way, 'Eh up, Jim, how are you diddling? Put a brew on before we go for a pint.'

I had chatted casually to him for years, but I began to get to know him in Cornwall over Whit weekend in 1980. He arrived unexpectedly at the Climbers Club hut at Bosigran late on a Friday night. The hut was full of rather earnest CC members and guests making coffee, reading guidebooks and making plans for the weekend when the door was flung open.

'Evenin' all,' he announced to no one in particular in his characteristic nasal Lancastrian accent. 'A've always meant to come down 'ere. Joe used to in t'fifties but I always preferred t'Alps. Bugger Cornwall, I used to say – I'll leave it till I'm an old man. Well, 'ere I am.'

Even by my standards, Don in his late forties was fat and unfit, consuming huge quantities of beer every night. But he had come down to Cornwall to climb as well as booze. I watched him next day at Chair Ladder seconding South Face Direct. He climbed quickly, neatly and with immense co-ordination and agility given his condition. At the top he untied his bowline with a grunt of satisfaction.

'Well, 'ere I am.' Don Whillans decides to give Cornwall a once over.

'Can't get a Whillans harness big enough to fit these days.' He peered down the cliff at a mass of helmeted beginners being shepherded up an easy route. 'Bloody 'ell – an outbreak of Easter eggs!'

Don, probably relating to my own shape and bad habits as much as anything else, seemed to enjoy my company and rather to my surprise we climbed and drank together quite frequently over the next four years. Often it was in Cornwall, for which Don developed a real affection. On several occasions I went with Cass, Gemma and Becky to camp at Trevedra Farm above Sennen Cove. Here in the company of 'abandoned wives' like Hilary Nunn, Sue Carrington and Maggie Boysen, whose husbands were all off on Himalayan expeditions, Don and I enjoyed climbing and socialising. He lived in his VW camper, a slightly lonely, self-contained figure, who would stump across the field and sit chatting outside our tents, talking to the various children, and occasionally kicking a football around with them.

He particularly enjoyed the climbing at Chair Ladder and I went back with him again to do Diocese, the classic Very Severe of the cliff. It was a hot day and low tide. At the bottom of the cliff a flat ledge was revealed on which several young climbers of both sexes were sunbathing. Oblivious to their amazed stares Don stripped off completely and, like a little pink depth charge, dived into the still water and cavorted around like a five-year-old.

The onlookers were equally nonplussed twenty minutes later when, wearing only an ancient pair of grey flannel trousers, Don climbed the first short, steep chimney of Diocese, heaving his beer gut to one side to avoid the constrictions.

I led the crux, gibbering on a high step and long reach on to a steep slab. 'I'll never do it like that,' Don muttered to himself as I lurched precariously upwards. But seconding he followed the pitch in a flash. I was impressed.

'I didn't do the first bit,' he explained, 'I just climbed up the chimney till I could reach the big 'olds and swing out.' I had done the climb twice before and it had never occurred to me that it could be outwitted like this. Don's ability to lateral think his way out of trouble must have got him out of many far more serious situations than this one. There were only two occasions when he found seconding me a problem. Once at Chatsworth Edge in Derbyshire he fell off an overhang, to my consternation, as I was belaying him rather casually from above and had to lower him all the way to the ground. And once in Cornwall on Kenidjack Castle Cliff when I had led the beautiful

Don Whillans seconding the South Face Direct of Chair Ladder in 1980.

climb Saxon, Don had found the reaches between holds very awk-ward and I found myself in the strange position of giving one of the greatest British rock climbers a tight rope.

In 1984 Don arrived at Trevedra Farm tired and unwell. He had just returned from Broad Peak where Pete Thexton had been stricken with cerebral oedema after an unsuccessful summit bid and died before he could be brought down. Don was still distraught at what had hap-pened and for several nights he sat up late, endlessly reliving the events. He had found the whole expedition bewildering, for the leader, Doug Scott, had expected everyone to climb in independent pairs, warming up on smaller peaks and building up to Broad Peak, then K2. Don couldn't adjust to the new alpine-style ethics and felt that several of the climbers were treating the Karakoram Mountains as a mere playground, with little attempt to help or work with each other. He was upset and disillusioned. I wondered whether, deep down, he realised it was probably his last big expedition. Sadly, it had ended in almost the same way as his first. Then, on Masherbrum in 1957, Bob Downes had died from pulmonary oedema, an experience that had affected Don deeply.

I always found Don's long discourses fascinating. His down-to-earth assessments and understanding of Himalayan climbing and his real respect for the risks and dangers involved, were really helpful and enlightening, quite apart from the fascination of listening to first-hand accounts of historic climbs such as Annapurna South Face and at-tempts on Everest's South-West Face. Don was not well educated in the conventional sense but he had great powers of observation and understanding. If his opinions were sometimes somewhat inflexible they were at least based on vast experience. On many occasions in pubs, at film festivals or conferences or, as in Cornwall, sitting in a tent, he was a mine of information, more than willing to give others the benefit of his knowledge.

As well as his endless fund of anecdotes, there were his legendary one-liners that have become collector's items. Whillans jokes will, I hope, be retold as long as there are climbers to tell them. They stand for an age and attitude when the northern working-class underdog often had the last word over class and privilege. Delivered over a pint, with a pause for maximum effect and a long, unblinking stare from piercing blue eyes, Don could hold an audience spellbound. He was the best lecturer I have ever heard (but not the best after-dinner speaker who is undoubtedly Ian McNaught-Davis, 'Mac' to everyone who knows him). Don's lectures, whether to a small group of club climbers or huge audiences in Manchester Free Trade Hall, appeared to be completely off-the-cuff improvisations but they had all the timing of a natural actor.

At Buxton Don once topped the bill at the British Mountaineering Council Conference. As he started his 'Life and Times' lecture a streaker unexpectedly ran across the stage, to the audience's delight. Don was temporarily flabbergasted. 'Well, I'll be buggered!' Then, seeing the funny side of it, he added quickly, 'And so will 'e if I catch 'im!'

Early in the lecture he showed an old black and white snapshot of a large group of walkers on a Derbyshire railway station. 'You may wonder why I've included this. [A pause.] That's me in the middle of the picture, but, over on the left corner is a girl I'd never spoken to at the time. [A longer pause.] That's my wife Audrey. [An even longer pause.] Which just goes to show that danger lurks when you least expect it . . .'

One evening at the Royal in Hayfield, Don was as usual entertaining a table of friends and hangers-on. Nazir Sabir, the well-known Pakistani climber who had made the first ascent of the West Ridge of K2, was visiting the country and was introduced to Don, one of his heroes. Don looked at him. 'Nazir, eh? I knew a guy called Wazir, but he's gone now!'

Whillans's penchant for weak puns (which reached its height in his nickname for the German expedition impresario, Dr Karl Herligkoffer, as Dr Stirlingscoffer) was equalled only by his ability to debunk pretension. A famous riposte was to a telegram sent by Chris Bonington when Don was stranded in Bombay waiting for the ship bringing the Annapurna equipment, which had broken down. Chris offered to fly out 'to pull strings'. 'The only useful string 'e could pull would be a bloody great big one attached to the ship.' On a walk-in to the Garhwal Don was accosted by a pilgrim dressed only in a loincloth and carrying a begging bowl. 'I suppose you're on some kind of sponsored walk?' he grumbled, grudgingly parting with a rupee.

In the late summer of 1984 Don rang me up at home. ''Ave you done that Dream of White Horses? Because every other bugger has.' I hadn't despite several visits to Wen Zawn on Craig Gogarth over the years that had been foiled by crowds or rain or cowardice. A Dream of White Horses is one of the very great Welsh climbs. Although only graded HVS 4c, it crosses an extremely impressive slab in an imposing position. 'We'll do a last ascent then,' Don chuckled as he rang off.

We arranged to meet and I drove him over from Mo and Jackie's to Anglesey. 'Go up to South Stack café,' instructed Don. 'I fancy a brew and the walk over to the crag.' It was a typical late summer day, mellow, slightly misty light and a calm sea. In midweek with no need to hurry it was early afternoon before we scrambled down to the abseil point at the top of Wen. 'Aye aye, someone's here before us.'

Despite a rope in place, Don preferred to solo, scrambling easily down to the stance at the top of the first pitch which we avoided due to high tide. I followed, pleased that Don's confidence seemed to rub off on me. When I had done Wen several years previously, I had found the whole place overpoweringly frightening.

On the stance a climber recognised Don and was mildly embarrassed. He was belaying a young lad trying to lead the second pitch and struggling with the crux moves, oblivious of watchers. Gripped, he advanced, retreated, and advanced once more. Don was quite happy to sit on the belay ledge smoking my cigarettes. 'Up and down like a bride's nightie,' he chuckled at the unfortunate's performance.

Number two was getting embarrassed. 'Come on, let's jack it in – you're obviously not going to do it and there's a couple here waiting.'

'Tell them to piss off,' was the response.

'You wouldn't say that if you knew who it was!'

Eventually he gave up in disgust and it was our turn. After some inner quaking I set off. Don eyed me intently as I started the hard moves. 'You know, I've been thinking. You're not really the right shape for climbing.' It was as good an incentive as any and I climbed the pitch quite easily after that. Don followed with that quick and delicate footwork that once again made me aware of what a good climber he had once been.

The next pitch is the easiest and Don offered to lead through. He took a small supply of nuts and Friends. 'You won't believe this, but I've never used these gadgets before.' He didn't then either, for he paused before the only hard move, soon after the beginning of the pitch, and expertly flicked a tape sling over a spike. Then he climbed straight through to the final belay, about thirty metres without a runner.

As I removed the sling I was aware of two more climbers a long way below and to my left climbing Concrete Chimney. They looked across apprehensively, as well they might. If I came off I would perform a colossal pendulum that could skittle them both into oblivion. I tried not to think about it and climbed with great care across to Don. 'Had you worried, didn't I? But I knew you'd be okay.'

The last pitch looked mindblowing, a bottomless set of slabs and overhangs perched above a huge void with, far below, the sea sucking and surging into the back of Wen Zawn. The hardest move is a long step down and it is protected by a peg from which hung tattered bits of sling.

'I think I'll give myself a back rope when I second it,' said Don, weighing up the possibilities of a fall over the overhangs below. I teetered nervously across the wall. The climbing was actually sur- prisingly easy but nerve-racking. Great hand and footholds seemed to be stuck to the parent rock as if by a careless model-maker who had lost interest in his work, but somehow it all held together. I worked my way into a final steep corner that led to the top. Suddenly and rather unexpectedly I found myself stepping left and on to flat ground. Done it!

The little figure of Don was still stuck on the middle of the wall waiting patiently while I constructed a solid belay. Then he climbed quickly to the peg, announced that he couldn't be bothered to mess around, unclipped and climbed across so quickly I had a job taking the rope in. But there was no mistaking his pleasure as he sat smoking and watching me coil the ropes up. 'That was just the kind of route I like these days: long enough to get into but not too hard.' He sat in contented silence watching the sea and the sky. In the still early evening the lighthouse of South Stack winked feebly in broad daylight. 'Come on,' said Don, 'I've got a morbid fear of dehydration. They'll be open by the time we get to Holyhead.'

I saw Don twice more after that. Once was in Hayfield. He was sitting on the wall in the car park early on an autumn evening, pint in hand.

'What's up, Don? You'll catch pneumonia out here.' He looked old and suddenly rather sad.

'I'll be in soon. I was just thinking – it all began in this car park back in the forties. The bus used to drop us off and we'd go for longer and longer walks. One thing led to another . . . but it all started here.'

We stood for a bit in silence and I went back to the bar.

In the spring of 1985 there was a Climbers Club dinner and disco at the Marquis of Granby near Hathersage. Cass and I drove over from Sheffield for the disco and walked into the hotel. A familiar figure clad in a leather jacket sat at a table, pint in hand and with a large motorcycle crash helmet on the floor. 'Aye aye, it's Jim and the Giraffe (this was Don's affectionate nickname for Cass) – I'm glad you're here because I was coming over to stay at your place tonight. Now I can leave the bike here.' Yes, and I can drive you back out tomorrow, you lazy little sod, I thought but didn't say. He was on good form and the pint glasses soon stacked up in front of him. It was a quiet evening and we left reasonably early. I wasn't drinking, in an effort to get fit for a forthcoming trip to South America.

'Aye, it's a pity it didn't work out, I could have fancied a trip to Peru.' Don had been invited to come as well, but was already going to the Dolomites.

Next morning we drove back to the Marquis of Granby and watched Don start up his big bike. 'Have a good trip, Jim. Take care. Do you fancy Cornwall again when you get back?' He pulled the helmet over his head and revved the bike.

'See you, Don.' I drove out of the car park and through my wing mirror caught a glimpse of the stocky little figure pulling away in the opposite direction. 'An odd life Don's got,' I reflected to Cass. 'He just seems to spend it going from place to place for no real reason.'

Cass laughed. 'Exactly like you! . . . I didn't think Don looked very well.'

13

BREAKING THE
HABIT OF A
LIFETIME

ONE OF the first climbing books I ever owned was *The Untrodden Andes* by C. G. Egeler and T. de Booy. It was given to me by my Uncle Harold at Christmas 1957 and I still have it. It describes the adventures of a small Dutch expedition to the Cordillera Blanca in Peru, with the great French climber Lionel Terray. I remember being amazed that just three people could actually go and explore and climb in such large and remote mountain ranges. But I have to say that until 1985 the Andes had never held much appeal to me compared with the Himalaya. The exception was Patagonia with its great granite spires which I would still dearly love to visit sometime.

Since the first Barnaj expedition Geoff Tier and I had maintained our casual friendship in the normal climber's way. Long silences were broken by odd days climbing, the occasional trip to Wales or Scotland, visits to Reading or Sheffield. Geoff had a friend from the Reading Climbers Club, Andy Maskrey, who was living in Lima. On several occasions Geoff had suggested an expedition to Peru. I had made desultory encouraging noises but not given it much thought.

But in 1985 Geoff was determined to go. Not having been on a proper trip since 1981 probably gave me the impetus to get involved and for the first time I found the idea of going west, not east, from Heathrow an exciting one. Where exactly we would be going was a bit of a problem, for both of us fancied doing something new, yet anything left to do in Peru would be either desperately hard or dangerous or both. Could there be anything remote enough to have been overlooked?

Geoff has, as I have tried to explain before, an enviable knack of Finding Things Out. What's more, he then Does Something About Them. As I lack both these attributes almost entirely I let him get on with it, knowing that my long-standing flair for being led astray would soon come to the fore.

So it was that Geoff's diligent research in the libraries of the Alpine Club and the Royal Geographical Society came up with three possibilities. I can't now remember the other two, but Al Rouse, Sheffield's resident Andean expert, vetted all three and unhesitatingly recommended we visited the little-known Cordillera Apolobamba in the south-eastern corner of Peru.

This range of mountains (sounding like a Latin American dance band – and fitting in well with *Trango* and what Don Whillans always referred to as 'Aye-aye, aye, aye Kongur') is some 130 kilometres north-east of Lake Titicaca on the Bolivian border. Geoff had stumbled upon its existence by the merest chance. Bored stiff in the RGS Library he had been through the entire South American mountain volumes when, on an adjoining table, he flipped idly through a bulky volume left by some other reader. It was a Boundary Commission Report surveying the exact location of the Peru/Bolivia border. There in a series of old black and white photographs were the mountains of the Apolobamba that defined part of the disputed border. This dry and dusty document was written by none other than the legendary Lieutenant-Colonel P. N. Fawcett who in the summer of 1925, accompanied by his son Jack and another Englishman called Raleigh Rimell, had left the last outpost of civilisation on the edge of an almost entirely unexplored region in the Central Brazilian Plateau in an attempt to find a lost city in the Matto Grosso. None of them was ever seen or heard of again, and their disappearance gave rise to immense and largely fanciful speculation as to their fate. Whatever it was, Colonel Fawcett's work now stood us in good stead.

Further research showed that although most of the mountains had been climbed, mainly by Swiss parties from the Bolivian side, one mountain, Palomani Tranca, actually straddled the border and had no record of an ascent. That would probably be our main objective but from the Peruvian side there would be plenty of scope for new routes on previously climbed mountains.

From Lima Andy Maskrey confirmed the feasibility of our plans. Andy, formerly a town planner like Geoff, had lived there for five years employed in the running of a disaster agency that advised and helped with a wide variety of Peru's all too pressing problems: earthquakes, poverty, shanty towns, floods, irrigation, medical aid

Geoff Tier, explorer, town planner and eccentric.

etc. If Andy was used to disasters, I thought, he should be able to cope with the two that were about to descend on him.

We obtained grants from the Mount Everest Foundation and the British Mountaineering Council. We originally planned on a four-man team, but Paul Nunn, our first choice, was already committed elsewhere and Don Whillans was planning a visit to the Alps. In the end we decided that three would have to do, though we knew that Andy had a girlfriend who would come with us to Base Camp at least.

At the end of June Geoff and I flew out of Heathrow. We had to change at Caracas where our connecting flight to Lima was delayed. All the passengers were transferred to the Sheraton Hotel where an impromptu eating contest was held. Unaware that some meals were free and the rest to be paid for a near-riot ensued when hotel staff tried to charge the passengers at the end of a long, hot day. It was clearly the airline's fault for making no attempt to explain the rules. It was our first experience of a full-scale Latin American cock-up, with emotions running high. I found it very amusing, and also a good way of fine-tuning our rusty senses that from now on would be tested on every occasion for the slightest possibility of a rip-off.

As if to remind me of what I had been missing since our overland drive to India, at Caracas airport I was treated to a spectacular display of Geoff Tier at his priceless, eccentric, infuriating worst. As we checked in and approached the x-ray machine, Geoff discovered that some sachets of shampoo he had stolen from the toilets on the DC10 had leaked all over his hand baggage. Calmly he sat down in the middle of the shuffling queue, and unruffled by the presence of several security guards wielding automatic rifles, proceeded to clean everything he possessed. Soon a slimy mass of used tissues, cameras, lenses, films, wallet, toothbrushes, passport and boarding card were scattered all over the floor. Passengers skidded past as if on skateboards and the flinty-eyed guards prodded him with their rifles. 'For Christ's sake, Geoff,' I muttered in a paroxysm of frustration and apprehension, 'let's get on the bloody plane before you're arrested.'

'Just hang on for a few more minutes. You've got to show these people who's boss and not get rattled by them.'

Lima is a vast sprawl that appears to have been built on some kind of grand design that has long since been abandoned. It has the defeated air of a city that is past its best. Great dual carriageways are pitted with craters and burst water mains. Buildings decay and in the uniform grey drabness you could be forgiven for thinking you had landed in Warsaw or Moscow.

Andy had met us at the airport. Small, dark and initially rather shy, he looked appalled at the two huge trunks, remnants from the Kongur expedition into which we had packed everything. We thought we were travelling amazingly lightly but Andy's lifestyle had a frugality that took some getting used to. Chepi, his girlfriend (now his wife), was half Indian. She found everything we said or did hilarious. She spoke almost no English and Andy had his work cut out translating our frequently inane comments as well as giving us a crash course in all things Peruvian.

Despite a visit to César Moralis at the Instituto Peruano del Deporte we couldn't get a decent map of the Cordillera Apolobamba. César Moralis is Peru's equivalent of Derek Walker, Chris Bonington, Lord Hunt and Audrey Salkeld rolled into one (an incongruous thought). His knowledge of the Andes is second to none and we spent a delightful hour in his office listening to his stories about the famous climbers he had met during his long and active life. We promised to send him a full expedition report and left with his wishes of good luck, but no map.

We also popped into the British Embassy to inform them of our plans but mainly to assure them that, in the event of an accident, we were not expecting them to provide a helicopter rescue service, which some tourists apparently take as being an embassy function. While we were there we first heard vague details that two British climbers, Simon Yates and Joe Simpson, had just flown home after a horrific accident and self-rescue epic by Simpson, who had crawled down a glacier with a badly broken leg after falling in a crevasse. It reminded me of our arrival at another British Embassy, in Islamabad, years before, to hear a remarkably similar story about Doug Scott on the Ogre. But it gave us a stern reminder that with just three of us we would be very vulnerable in a remote area if anything went wrong.

At last we were ready to go and carted our by now ludicrously heavy trunks to the bus station. At least they were highly unlikely to be stolen, for Geoff and I could barely manage to lift one together. Unwittingly we had found the perfect way of deterring thieves and from then on we were more relaxed at railway stations, airports and hotels. A long overnight coach ride to Arequipa was followed by another night on a train. In the space of a few hours we were going from sea level to about 4000 metres and for the first but certainly not last time in my life I took Diamox tablets as a precautionary measure against pulmonary or cerebral oedema. These had recently become available and are a sensible precaution if altitude is being gained quickly. In Peru, as in Tibet and Sinkiang, one can get to quite high altitudes on buses or trains. This is obviously unnatural in itself, so I can't see any reason why Diamox should not be used to help offset any ill effects.

The train to Puno skirted Lake Titicaca in the bright early morning light. The huge stretch of water is the highest navigable lake in the world and a ferry service runs to Bolivia across its breadth. Surrounding the lake is the altiplano, the high, windswept plateau of Peru and Bolivia. As the train traversed the glinting lakeside, my spirits rose. In the distance mountains were silhouetted against a cloudless sky. In the foreground banks of reeds stretched into the lake's clear, blue waters. I was captivated and the slight depression that had held me since arriving in Lima was swept away.

Puno, clinging to the shores of Lake Titicaca, is an attractive little city with ornate squares and a rather forbidding cathedral. Here at the landing stage was the present-day steamer. The original one was built in Hull in 1862, sailed to Peru, dismantled on the coast, hauled bit by bit up to Puno and reassembled on the lake. We checked into a drab little hotel and, even with the Diamox, almost had heart failure carting the trunks up to our rooms. Despite the cloudless sky, Puno was bitingly cold out of the sun. In June the temperatures at night are well below freezing, though the best weather in the Peruvian Andes is in June and July. If this sounds confusing, it is.

We spent a few days in Puno mainly to acclimatise and sort out transport for the next stage towards our mountains. The nearer we got, however, the more elusive they became and the vaguer the information grew. (On one occasion we were told we had come to the wrong country.) We were by now totally dependent on Andy's fluent Spanish and Chepi's native Quechua language. Without them Geoff and I would have long since foundered, for in Peru we were gringos, not sahibs. Eventually Andy found out that we could catch a lorry from the nearby town of Juliaca which would take us most if not all the way, and we set off in a decrepit taxi.

Juliaca ranks with some of the very nastiest places I've ever been to. It knocks Bethesda into a cocked hat and makes Skardu airport in Baltistan seem almost pleasant. Only an awful little collection of houses at the foot of the Skora La in Baltistan rivals the position as the place I would least like to be exiled to. We found a hideously dirty hotel and hired a room next to the lavatory. The bitter cold saved us from the ghastly smells that I knew lay dormant in the sub-zero temperatures. Andy and Chepi shared a bed for warmth more than anything else while Geoff and I each shivered in solitude.

With no incentive to lie in we left early and found the lorry that eventually took us, our luggage and what seemed like half the population of Juliaca for a prolonged and apparently pointless ride round and round the gruesome streets. After an eternity, the driver managed to escape from the city's magnetic orbit and headed out on the open road, across the altiplano towards the distant hills on the north-eastern shores of Lake Titicaca.

We stopped occasionally, once at a small village by the side of a subsidiary lake where we were sold small, delicious fried fish. Later we stopped at a satanic transport café in a grim village of grey, uniform drabness. Overhead the sky darkened and we started grinding up a never-ending series of hairpins on a dirt road that deteriorated by the mile. Snow started to fall. A tarpaulin was slung over the back of the lorry, under which we huddled next to impassive Indians who had seen it all before. At last, in pitch darkness, we stopped in a full-blown blizzard, in the middle of nowhere. A light glowed and everyone made their way to a farm building. We followed and found ourselves in a large, stone-floored room. All around us were unconscious Indians. There didn't seem to be anything else to do, so we dug out our sleeping-bags and, in a barrage of snoring that made Chris Bonington's best efforts seem like the merest whisper of a far-away sea breeze, we too fell into oblivion.

In the morning the storm had cleared and we emerged blinking in the blinding light to a white landscape dominated by the long whale-back of Ananea, the mountain that gives the nearby town its name. This was a recent development, for the town used to be called Poto, which means arsehole. Not unnaturally, the inhabitants had decided to change it. I felt they were mistaken. After a night in Ananea Andy and Chepi managed to sort out a lorry that would take us to Lake Suches at the foot of the Apolobamba range. It was a brilliant frosty morning. Under a huge, clear blue sky the lorry followed a tenuous dirt road past an impressive mountain, Callejon, that had a look of north-west Scotland about it. Then as we slowly breasted a gentle ridge, the Cordillera Apolobamba came into sight. We turned off the tracks and headed straight out over the frozen altiplano, incongruously driving over terrain which seemed as rough as Kinder or Bleaklow but that didn't appear to trouble the driver at all. On one occasion he stopped suddenly and drew our attention to a herd of vicuna, small, elegant relatives of the llama, whose fine wool has caused these animals to become almost extinct. They are now a protected species.

As the mountains took form we all heaved a sigh of relief. They were obviously worth coming all this way for, and on first glance seemed within our capabilities to climb. Soon Palomani Tranca itself was identified. It was rockier than its neighbour, Palomani Grande, and at 5633 metres a bit lower. It was hardly the find of the decade but looked a worthwhile peak to bag before we got cracking on all the hard new routes waiting to be done. This was rampant optimism, as it turned out.

Suddenly we found ourselves at the top of another ridge and looking down at the still, deep, blue waters of Lake Suches. The other side of the lake was Bolivia. It was wild, desolate and incredibly beautiful. Below was a tumbledown farm. An amazed Indian stared in disbelief as we disembarked. Dogs growled and snarled. Andy and Chepi befriended the farmer and explained our reason for being here. He seemed an honest man and soon he had shown us the best place to camp, about 400 metres away, just above the lake by a small pool, and had offered to look after our Base Camp while we were on the mountain.

We ferried the dreaded trunks down to our site and as the afternoon sun lengthened the shadows we got ourselves organised. At six p.m. dusk fell rapidly and the temperature with it. Twelve hours of darkness and a light snow shower later I was roused from my slumbers by a clopping of horses' hooves. I just had time to take a photo of a horseman wearing a poncho and bowler hat, trotting along the snow-covered shore against the ultramarine of the lake. This was it – the authentic feel of Peru. Suffused in the satisfied afterglow of ethnic consciousness I became aware, a few minutes later, of a high-pitched buzzing like an irate hornet. Poking my head out of the tent I was surprised and not a little dismayed at the sight of another Indian, wearing jeans, an old leather jacket, and riding an all-too-modern moped. He didn't get his picture taken. Where had he come from and where was he going? Who knows?

Our first priority was to get to the foot of the mountain. A simple task, we thought. It was about five miles to the end of the lake and the foot of the Palomani group. Visibility was perfect, yet we managed to get lost carrying light loads to a prospective Advance Base below the glacier that separated Palomani Tranca from Palomani Grande. We had left the rough path past the lake far too early and walked up the wrong hillside. Too late we realised that an unseen valley lay between us and the foot of the mountain. We lost and regained height miserably and eventually dropped our loads off with relief in a beautiful little high pasture underneath 'our' mountain. Then we slogged back – the right way this time – along the lakeside, passing another even more ramshackle farm halfway. A three-legged dog tried to kill us as we walked by. We got back to our tents as dusk fell, cursing our stupidity at a first day out in which we must have covered about fourteen miles at around 4500 metres. We were knackered.

That night was the start of the Great Petrol Stove saga. Geoff had brought his with him and it was the only stove we could get fuel for. I have always loathed petrol stoves, seeing them as semi-controlled explosions at best and almost completely beyond human control. Peruvian petrol is pretty rough and for the entire time at Base Camp and on the mountain, meals were occasions of high stress. On countless occasions holes would be burned in the groundsheet (*my* groundsheet) and frequently the whole stove would be ejected like a fireball from the tent. I was morbidly convinced that we would end up cremating ourselves on some lonely snow slope, a little beacon of flame that would be visible for miles and miles, glimmering briefly in the clear night air. That it didn't happen was, I am sure, only due to my constantly nagging Geoff, whose cavalier attitude to the stove was almost as frightening as its erratic performance.

We had one rest day before all four of us packed huge loads and walked very slowly up to our prospective campsite. We passed the halfway farm with justifiable trepidation and made the interesting discovery that whereas the three-legged dog was utterly fearless when confronted with ski sticks (even when rammed halfway down its throat) a badly aimed stone, or even the miming of picking one up, would send it cringing for shelter. I was wearing my red salopettes from the Kongur expedition and later we heard from 'our' farmer that the inhabitants of the lakeside farm were terrified at the sight of a portly red giant lumbering across their land holding what appeared to be two spears. Apparently they thought I was a reincarnate god. We all make mistakes.

We regained our high pasture and pitched two little tents in an idyllic pastoral landscape with the twin peaks of Palomani Grande and Palomani Tranca framed in the tent doorway. A herd of alpaca grazed around us. Like the vicuna they are related to the llama. We found out later that all the alpacas in the valley belonged to the same *collectivo* and that the wool would eventually be shipped to a firm in Liverpool.

We spent the next day walking up the valley and exploring a way on to the glacier separating the two peaks. I have to admit it was I who insisted that the obvious way to climb the mountain was up the glacier to a col and then turn right up the rocky north ridge to the summit. Now we were at the foot of the mountain it seemed so straightforward we thought we could do it, up and down, in one day. As the weather was fine and apparently settled, and as we seemed to be reasonably fit and well, there was no reason not to have a go the next day.

Before dawn Geoff burned another hole in the groundsheet and after a brew and some Ready Brek we set out at the very first glimmer of light, stumbling over the frozen, bumpy tussocks of moss surrounding the tents and picking our way towards the innocuous little glacier that led to the col. A short icefall barred access to the upper slopes but this could be turned on the right by what we hoped would be an easy scramble between the lateral moraine and the retaining north wall of Palomani Tranca.

It was one of those days. Like alpine novices we stumbled and bumbled upwards, finding every possible obstacle in our path. We were forced on to some steep, dusty, glacier-worn slabs and the three of us picked separate ways until we were all stuck. Belatedly we roped up and after wasting at least a couple of hours we set foot on the glacier. It was our first introduction to Andean snow conditions. Despite the combined effects of cold and midday sun almost vertically overhead the snow was deep, unconsolidated powder that concealed a maze of crevasses. For two more hours we moved slowly up the undulating slopes, through another broken section and eventually on to some easier, featureless slopes. Geoff led, with me, the biggest and heaviest, in the middle. As we gained height I began to realise that we were still not much more than halfway to the col. There seemed to be no chance of climbing the ridge above without a bivouac, and my spirits, which had never been very high, fell steadily.

In the middle of a long, diagonal traverse Geoff broke through the surface and a quite audible tinkling of ice particles seemed to come from beneath my feet. Suddenly I was gripped. 'Geoff – I think we're playing with fire here.' With this inappropriate analogy the three of us gathered uneasily in the snow and sat down to discuss the situation. Geoff initially wanted to carry on but I was adamant in my cowardice. 'I just don't think we've got a cat in hell's chance of getting up this thing today and in any case I think this glacier is suicidal.' Rather like on the Koksel Glacier four years earlier, we were following parallel crevasse systems that all three of us could conceivably fall into simultaneously. Unlike the Koksel Glacier, however, this had far more small crevasses and it was only luck that stopped us going in. Andy agreed with me and in the early afternoon we decided to retreat.

As usual once the decision was made it seemed rather a feeble one and we guiltily retraced our steps. But this time we crossed the glacier to end up on its far bank, a much easier way, which showed up our poor route-finding of the morning. Crestfallen and ashamed of ourselves, we tramped back to Chepi who had been watching our progress, or lack of it, and had got a brew on for us. It hadn't been too long a day but we were all quite tired. Two things were obvious. The first was that we had grossly underestimated the scale and difficulty of the mountain and second that the glacier approach was not on. If we couldn't find a safer route we might not get up the mountain. I felt vaguely outraged that such an unimpressive hill could rebuff us so effortlessly. Later Geoff and I lay in our tent drinking a moody cup of coffee laced with whisky. 'The trouble with easy mountains, Geoff, is that they don't ever seem to be easy enough.' I had a vision of everyone in Sheffield laughing at our inept performance and slowly drifted off to sleep.

In the morning we all woke with a renewed sense of determination. There had to be a better route. Geoff set off to explore a long ridge south of our Advance Base that led to a junction with the West Ridge high above us. Andy and Chepi walked higher up the valley, and I climbed a hill behind our camp to get a good view of the whole mountain. Through the 200 mm zoom lens of my Canon F1 I examined the West Ridge of Palomani Tranca and identified a long and hideous-looking scree slope immediately above our camp which led directly to the crest of the West Ridge. It would certainly cut a big chunk off Geoff's route, but I couldn't really work out what the Ridge itself was like. I could see more than one potential summit, and the top section looked as though it could be much more difficult than we had suspected.

I descended quickly. Andy and Chepi returned at much the same time and we waited, with mounting anxiety, for Geoff. It was almost dark before he stumbled in, absolutely shattered, to tell us what he had discovered. His ridge had indeed been a long one and it had taken all morning and into the afternoon to get to the point that my prospective scree slope would reach more directly. From the crest of the ridge Geoff could see the upper section of the mountain at close quarters. He reported the existence of yet another possible summit, this one well off the main ridge to the south and made up of ice flutings. Geoff had descended an appalling series of blind gullies and dangerous scree slopes before eventually emerging just below the glacier and retracing our steps of the day before. He hadn't spotted my possible line of ascent and didn't know if there was an easy way through a rotten rock band that barred access to the ridge.

After several brews he suddenly brightened up. 'Did you see the condor? I got some great photos.'

I was consumed with envy. This massive bird whose wingspan can exceed four metres is *the* symbol of the Andes. I had never seriously thought that we would see one and imagined that, like the Scottish eagle, they were very rare. Apparently Geoff's condor had circled up from below him and then soared effortlessly across to hover around the top of the hill I was climbing. And I hadn't noticed it. Bugger.

Geoff needed and deserved a rest day, so while Andy and Chepi returned to Base Camp and brought up some more food and another bottle of contraband whisky, I decided to explore the scree slope. I took a light load of climbing gear to drop off at whatever highpoint I reached and started up the interminable slightly muddy scree, all too conscious of Geoff lounging outside the tent observing my snail-like progress.

After about three hours of misery, during which my rest stops became increasingly frequent and my uphill progress progressively less, I was rewarded by the growing proximity of the broken buttress through which I hoped there would be an easy way. To my delight the scree slope narrowed into a broken, easy gully cutting through the cliff. There was no difficulty or danger at all and I climbed until I could see the way clear to a snow-field I knew Geoff had traversed the previous day. I dropped the climbing gear under a small overhang and, delightfully unladen, slid and clattered down in about half an hour. Andy and Chepi returned and we decided to go for it the following day. We would take a tent and try and do the climb in two or three days.

We soon reached the cache of gear I had left and divided it between us, then, slower now, set off grinding interminably up the long snow slope at the top of the gully. Geoff was certain that he had seen a good place for a tent when he had crossed over the ridge. As the afternoon wore on we gained height until we could see over my little hill and the view opened right up. At last we found the perfect site, a snowy basin sheltered in between two rocky outcrops.

As usual, darkness was upon us before we expected it and Geoff once more gave way to his pyromania, this time cooking a wonderful mess of Smash with chillis, cheese and tuna fish mixed in. While he coped with the leaping flames, I gazed out at the afterglow left by the setting sun. The snow slope turned a lurid orange. Behind, in a velvet haze, the peaks of the Cordillera Real in Bolivia were coral pink against the evening sky. Soon the temperature plummeted and we tried to get some sleep.

Despite being tired, the combination of apprehension and anticipation kept me restlessly tossing and turning in the cramped tent. This, combined with a strong smell of petrol, made for a grim night. I was relieved when at four a.m. Geoff once more did battle with the stove.

By six we were stumbling around outside the tent, strapping on crampons and knocking frozen snow off our ice axes. In the half light of dawn the stars were fading in the sky. There was no sign of anyone else in the world, I thought, then realised that away to the west was a faint orange glow in the night air. It must be the lights of the goldmine at Ananea. Somehow it made the loneliness more, not less. It was numbingly cold and as soon as possible we set off, leaving the little blue igloo tent nesting in the hollow. I wondered what we would have done when we next returned to it, and concentrated on putting one foot in front of the other without falling over.

About fifty metres above us was the crest of the East Ridge. A slope of perfect névé led to it up which we cramponed with a surge of optimism. This was tempered on our arrival at the top when we hit the normal bottomless powder snow. Only by moving along the precise crest could we rely on reasonable going – a metre either side and we were in up to our thighs. We were all too aware that if the snow conditions on the Ridge itself deteriorated it would take days, not hours, to get along the couple of miles between us and the summit.

As we moved off unroped along the Ridge, the first rays of sun exploded from over the summits directly in front of us. It was almost impossible to see what lay ahead, but behind the view was impressive. Beyond Lake Suches the Cordillera Real caught the sun. Behind again the first anvil clouds rose from the depths of the Amazon basin, clouds that encroached as the day wore on but never quite made it as far as the Apolobamba.

Geoff pulled steadily ahead, but stopped frequently to take photos, allowing us nearly to catch up. The Ridge gained height slowly, but at last we stopped underneath a steep snow slope that turned to ice.

'Let's rope up while we can.' We used a single 8.8 mm rope, fifty metres long. It was the absolute minimum we dared bring in our desire to keep the weight down. Geoff led, as he was to all day, gradually trending up and to his left to belay near a tottering spike. Below, the Ridge fell steeply away to the glacier. Above was the gleam of ice, up which Geoff climbed with studied care. He disappeared from sight and the rope ran out so I followed, hoping he would find a belay. The slope was convex and soon I could see neither Geoff above nor Andy below. At last, after we had all been moving together over steep but straightforward ground, Geoff came into sight.

'What's the score? Can you see anything? Are you on top?'

'Well, yes and no,' came the reply. 'Wait till you get here and see for yourself.'

At last the angle eased and we plodded up to where Geoff sat, and tried to take in the long-awaited revelation. We were just below the lowest of the four potential summits. Three hundred metres to the south was Geoff's fluted peak, which was not much, if any, higher than we were. Ahead was the summit ridge. It looked everything a summit ridge should. About 200 metres away and some fifty metres higher than the point on which we stood was an impressive black fang topped with snow. It was the real summit. There was no doubt about that. But between us and it was a steep, subsidiary gendarme. There was also no doubt that we would have to follow the very crest of the ridge all the way (despite a lunatic proposal from Geoff to traverse around the gendarme on to its steep North Face). We sat down and stared at the ridge.

'It looks a bit gripping.'

'I suppose we do have to do it?'

'It should be okay – let's have a look anyway.'

'At least we ought to get an article in *High* magazine now.'

We descended to leave our sacks on the fore-summit, and set off downhill to the little col below the gendarme. I belayed Geoff by sitting astride the ridge with one foot in Peru and the other in Bolivia and my axe buried to the head. Andy stayed well behind me and Geoff, now on steep, bottomless powder snow, carved a trench to the point where the angle steepened and he could kick huge bucket steps. He stopped halfway and I floundered up to join him. The belays were illusory and I doubt, had any one of us fallen, whether the others could have held him.

At the top of the gendarme we stopped again and looked at the final pinnacle. Mercifully the descent didn't appear to be too bad but the final fifty metres to the top looked horrifying. Once again we moved cautiously downhill and paused on a similar little col below the last ridge.

'Quite a place, isn't it?' Geoff set off and once again I pretended to belay him. Just as I did on Scottish winter climbs, I oscillated between concentrating on Geoff, admiring the view and suffering great waves of suppressed panic as I imagined the consequences of a fall. Andy and I scarcely spoke. The summit seemed as far away as ever as Geoff announced he had found a rock belay (the only one on the entire climb). I found him tied to a couple of small wires slotted into some protruding slivers of shaky rock. Above him tottering bookshelves of similar rock led upwards. Climbing with great care, Geoff pressed on and eventually, after a long silence, announced matter-of-factly that he was at the top. I followed, finding the last steep step decidedly awkward and already gripped at the prospect of the descent.

Geoff had stopped a few feet from the summit. Andy arrived and Geoff moved up to the snowy crest. There was only room for one at a time to shuffle cautiously around, glancing uneasily down at the bounding drop below. We shook hands and I felt a huge grin coming on. Both Geoff and Andy were similarly afflicted and we revelled in the situation. For me it was the single best moment in twenty-six years of climbing. It was easily the most impressive summit I had ever been to (much smaller than the Old Man of Hoy) and for someone accustomed to spending most expeditions nearer the bottom than the top of the mountains I had come to climb, it broke the habit of a lifetime. It was just midday and we had six hours to get back to the tent.

Over in Bolivia (which was only a metre or so away) great cumulo-nimbus clouds rose into the blue sky. They posed no immediate threat but it did seem that the perfect days we had grown accustomed to might not last for ever. Away on the fore-summit the tiny dots of our rucksacks seemed a long way off. After about half an hour we prepared to descend.

This was much easier than I had feared, and we made such good time that Geoff and Andy were all for pressing right on down to Base Camp in one push. Outvoted on this, I told them in no uncertain terms what I thought of their barmy decision, then with a great surge of energy that was a direct result of my ill temper, I set off again and led all the way down.

We just made it through the rocky gully in the very last glimmer of daylight. Then it was just one foot in front of the other. The mountains turned indigo against the last faint stretch of light in the sky. I was moved almost to tears both by fatigue and by a profound satisfaction. At last the scree levelled out and next there was Chepi's big smile, the tent, a brew. Another brew. Stiff and almost asleep, Geoff and I repitched my tent. I crawled into my sleeping-bag. The end of an eighteen-hour day. Oblivion.

And there, perhaps, this particular story should end as well, but we were to spend another four weeks in Peru. While they were undoubt-edly more of a holiday than an expedition, they certainly did not lack incident. The day after we got down the weather broke and with it died the faint desire for another climb. We were fulfilled. Before we left I too spotted a condor. Honour was satisfied, we decided to go.

A big, fat boiled trout and a huge, tasty Peruvian potato on a tin plate, a cup of hot, fishy water swimming in grease from the trout to wash it down made a curious breakfast. We were sitting in a market-place in Huancane after a long night in a lorry carrying alpaca wool from the mountains. Two days had passed since our return to the farmhouse, during which we had moved in short stages towards Peru and civilisation. The previous evening in a scene that could have come straight out of *The Ascent of Rum Doodle* we had seen all our equipment transported from one end of a village to the other by four small children whose ages ranged from four to seven. They had used a wheelbarrow to do this job but I still felt a twinge of guilt about our exploitation of child labour.

Later we were dropped off in the ghastly suburbs of the dreaded Juliaca, and this time with no qualms at all we hired a man on a tricycle to pedal the two trunks to the centre. So far on the trip we had used aircraft, buses, taxis, wheelbarrows and tricycles which as far as I could see only left boats as a means of transport. This was soon to be remedied.

Before we left Puno we decided to visit the Isla Tequila in the middle of Lake Titicaca. It was a four-hour voyage across the still, intensely blue waters to the tiny island where we were given a genuinely warm and friendly welcome and billeted in what seemed to be someone's garden shed. That afternoon and all evening a festival was in progress and most of the inhabitants were paralytically drunk as they performed a long and complex variation on a maypole dance. There were superb views to Bolivia in the east where the huge mass of Illampu (6485 metres) dominated the horizon.

We returned in the same tumbledown wreck of a motor boat that had brought us. It was terribly overcrowded and a violent storm blew up. Apart from feeling sick and very cold, for none of us wore more than T-shirts and shorts, the boat was in real danger of sinking in the icy water, and started taking in water. The passengers baled frantically with anything that came to hand. We were forced to seek shelter for hours in reed beds. Eventually the squall cleared. Under a huge, full moon and chilled to the bone we chugged back through the now still waters to the lights of Puno. It was, by a long way, the most dangerous experience of the expedition, and judging from the ashen faces of all on board, a lot more than everyone else had bargained for, too. Trudging through the cold, deserted streets to our hotel I have never been so pleased to be on dry land. I am not a sailor.

After that, walking the Inca Trail was a pleasant anticlimax. A few days unwinding in Lima and it was time to say goodbye to Andy and Chepi who had done so much to make the trip a success. Not since the Trango Tower expedition had I felt such a sense of achievement. Still with big summit grins on our faces we flew back to Heathrow where Cass had come to meet us.

We pushed our laden airport trolleys towards the multi-storey car parks, delighted to be back in the cool, moist August air. 'What's the news, Cass? Anyone died since I've been gone?'

It was a flippant question, but Cass's face fell.

'Oh no, I wasn't going to tell you till we got home. It's Don, he died last week. A heart attack.'

14

B IS FOR BIRD, E IS FOR EGG

THIS TIME, Curran, I thought miserably, you're really out of your depth, both literally and metaphorically. Cold, wet and hugging the wet, black rubber bow of the inflatable, I tried to take in the fragmentary and horrifying visual stimuli that threatened to over-whelm me. Heaving, grey-green mountains of water, spray breaking and blowing from their crests; towering black beetling overhangs dripping slimy tendrils of seaweed; whirling waterspouts skidding over the surface, churning it to white froth; fulmars dodging and weaving around the waves. High above, two pale, anxious faces peered down; Howard and Steve preparing to abseil into the wildly pitching boat from their precarious stance thirty metres up. Their ropes blew uncontrollably, now almost snagging the prop shaft. Steve is almost down and we rise on a wave to meet him. 'Jump!' Too late, we descend all of ten metres and Steve, soaked by the next wave, is almost submerged. Water streams off the rocks – Now! – Quick! Steve half jumps, half dives and lands all over us in a tangle of limbs, ironmongery and ropes. Paddy at the helm, calmly manoeuvres the dinghy on the heaving swell. Howard arrives in similar confusion and we quickly back away from the rocks. Across the base of the cliff the others are jumping into the reserve boat. All aboard, though few of us have life-jackets. Chris opts for a long, lonely jumar up the fixed ropes to safety. Now we are out into the teeth of the wind and rain, gunning it for home and steering an intricate path through the breaking seas: under, over and round the shifting, rolling monsters, fear slowly abating and a deep primitive feeling of achievement takes its place as the seas diminish and we approach the shelter of Village Bay. Chris gets back equally soaked a couple of hours later. 'Another fine mess you've got me into,' I greet him on his return.

It was mid-August, 1987. A difficult time. Since my return from Peru in 1985 a whole lot had happened which I still found difficult to come to terms with. I had gone to K2 in the summer of 1986 when thirteen climbers died on the world's second highest mountain, including Al Rouse. My intense sorrow at his death, and all the lingering controversy surrounding the disasters of that summer had been a major crisis in my life, one I had tried to come to terms with in a book, *K2 Triumph and Tragedy* and a film. Now I had finished writing the book and was in limbo until its publication in October.

I half envied Brian Hall, who told me that he and Chris Bonington were going with a big team, led by the Lakeland climber Peter Whillance, to St Kilda, some forty miles west of the Outer Hebrides. It had been a long-standing but unrealistic goal of my own. Joe and Mo had been there, and talked of a huge, unclimbed cliff called Conachair. The original inhabitants used to live off seagulls and their eggs. It was now an army base but access was restricted and climbing banned. Typical of Chris to wangle his way into going, I had thought jealously, consoling myself with the fact that, as the world's worst sailor, a visit to St Kilda was probably best kept a fantasy. I had in any case made a promise to take Gemma and Becky to the Alps camping, walking and generally trying to spend more time with them to make up for the lost holidays of the last two years. Then Chris rang up . . .

Our trip to Chamonix was cut to a mere ten days. But there was brilliant walking around the Aiguilles, and I enjoyed the pleasure that Gemma and Becky obviously felt at their first encounter with big mountains. All too soon, it was time for a mad dash up the autoroutes through torrential thunderstorms to Calais. I dropped the girls off in Manchester and next day carried on up the M6 to Caldbeck and a jovial Chris, brimming with enthusiasm. Even now he and Wendy give the impression they are still on their honeymoon in their obvious delight in each other's company. I was pleased to see that Chris was far less prepared than I. I had managed to do a quick raid on a supermarket on the way up and had bought enough food for two people (myself and our boatman) to last three weeks, as per instructions. I was slightly appalled at how much I had brought but I knew we would have to be self-sufficient on St Kilda and it was better to be safe than sorry. Then Brian Hall arrived and I watched, awestruck, as box after box of provisions was loaded into the back of Chris's Volvo estate. One of us must be wrong.

Before we left Wendy told me with great glee that Chris had attended a course for businessmen on Inner Awareness and Self-Realisation and had had to list his failings. Impatience and easy loss of temper had topped the list. 'Just remind him when he does it and I'm sure he'll get better,' was her parting shot. Remembering Kongur I had little doubt that, unless Chris had undergone a radical transformation, I would spend quite a bit of the next three weeks being the guinea-pig for his as yet unproven management skills.

We arrived in Oban at midnight and, due to me holding the map upside down, drove straight past the hotel. 'By the way' – Chris suddenly adopted an air of studied innocence that put me on my guard – 'you don't happen to remember the name of the boat we're going over on, do you?'

Not so fast. 'Chris,' I replied firmly, 'you've never told me.'

'To be honest,' he admitted, 'I've not just forgotten its name, I can't remember who owns it or where we're expected to find it either.'

In light drizzle we drove round Oban, still unable to decipher the map. The only inhabitants not in bed were, naturally, drunk and though several gave us directions, neither of us managed to understand a word they said. Particularly not Chris, who confessed that whenever he asked anyone for directions he never bothered to listen to the reply. But it seemed a good omen that we eventually arrived at the hotel without actually losing our good humour. Brian, who had found it instantly, was in the bar, laughing as he told us that he had seen us sweep past with me studying the upside-down map and Chris peering at the wrong side of the road.

The next morning, 29th August, we found our boat, the *Charna*, without difficulty and met the rest of our team, minus Pete Whillance and Ian McMullan who were already on St Kilda completing a college field study of the islands. Mike Mortimer and Marjorie Allen I knew already, stalwarts of the Climbers Club and, even in their fifties, still incredibly keen rock climbers. So too was Howard Lancashire from Nottingham, whom I had been to Lundy with years before. His partner, Steve Boyden, was a new name and face to me, as was Paddy Frost, our invaluable boatman. Paddy is a Cornishman, a member of Bude Lifeboat and runs an outdoor activities centre. He had done some climbing and he and I were to team up. As I had just bought all our food without consulting him, I hoped we would see eye to eye. I need not have worried.

The *Charna* is a converted Scottish trawler. It looked to me to be slightly on the small side as we loaded a prodigious amount of kit on board, lashing our two inflatables to the deck. The voyage would take a full twenty-four hours, first through the Inner Isles up through the Minch and across to the Hebrides. Then through the Sound of Harris, separating North Uist from Harris, and into the open North Atlantic for the final forty miles to Hirta, the biggest island of the St Kilda group and only port in Village Bay. It sounded wonderful. Or it would have done were it not for a gale warning. I had brought several brands of seasick pill and Marjorie also had a variety that, she said, more or less guaranteed immunity. I took most of them well before we set off, in case they made me feel sick.

We left late in the afternoon, chugging out of Oban's picturesque dock below the strange Coliseum-like folly that incongruously dominates the town. Apart from the strong reek of diesel fuel and the general fishy smell you would expect of a converted Scottish trawler, it was all disconcertingly gentle. The coastline slipped past with a grey cottonwool cloudbase clinging to the hillsides. As dusk fell we hit the open sea and a gentle but increasing swell. We all sat in the wheelhouse and conversation gradually flagged. Mike Mortimer was the first to go below, returning almost immediately, pale and sweating. The boat hit a bigger wave and dropped into the trough beyond. Right then, I'm off to bed. Quickly I rushed below, spread my sleeping-bag on a bench and climbed in. Just in time. Lying flat I could just about cope with the sweeping, plunging movement. All night the boat heaved and crashed through the waves, the engine note throbbing its unvarying pitch into my brain. In the grey light of dawn a wretched Mike appeared on his way to the toilet (or 'heads', as I believe they are called on boats). He didn't make it. Indeed he appeared to be turning himself inside out into the galley sink. I pretended not to notice.

Chris seemed his normal cheerful self when he got up and went on deck clutching a batch of cameras. This time I pretended to be dead. The only problem was that I was racked by thirst and the desire to go to the lavatory. The latter couldn't be put off much longer and eventually I slid out of my pit and lurched to the bog, which one moment was just in front of me and the next bucked wildly out of reach. At last I managed to grab the door, pulled myself inside and was promptly violently sick. Oh God, get me out of here. Every time I tried to leave I was sick again. Eventually Chris's stentorian voice summoned me on deck. St Kilda was in sight. Big bloody deal. I slumped in the wheelhouse – too ill even to look. 'Come on now, Jim.' Chris was trying hard to be kind. 'You've got to film this.' By closing my eyes and doing it all by touch I got the camera ready, then lurched on the deck where a thin wire was all that protected me from the not unwelcome attraction of a watery grave. As the vast stacks of Stac an Armin and Stac Lee wheeled past, grim, battleship grey and guano-streaked, I tried to film between separate retches. Using the view-finder of the camera made things worse. Like so many before and after me I prayed for the dry land of Hirta, on which I would gladly spend the rest of my life. At long last the boat entered calmer waters. An army inflatable buzzed around us. Pete Whillance and Ian McMullan were on board and we shouted bits of news across the water. I had never met Pete before and was aware that his first impressions of me were not what I would have chosen. White as a sheet, with fragments of diced carrot still clinging to my fibre-pile jacket, I stumbled into the inflatable and five minutes later – the joy of it – I scrambled on to the great granite blocks of the small jetty that was the only structure that elevated Village Bay to the status of a dock. But within seconds this too started heaving and swaying as I failed to regain my shore legs.

We had thought that we would be camping. In fact we were to be billeted in the converted cottages run by the Nature Conservancy Council who manage the islands, which are owned by the National Trust for Scotland on behalf of the nation. The young warden, David Miller, had been worried that our activities might damage the unique flora and fauna he was there to protect, so he joined us after our evening meal to brief us on what we could and couldn't do. No climbing on the great stacks, the home of the huge bird colonies. I heaved a sigh of relief, for I had not relished the prospect of visiting those vast, vertical walls of bird shit, and hoped that other cliffs on the islands would be more amenable. No climbing on the island of Dùn, a spectacular promontory bounding the south side of Village Bay and cut off by a narrow channel. This was the home of the puffin colonies. We could see its jagged profile from the cottage window and it would have given superb climbing, but there was no way round it. We were asked to avoid removing any vegetation or disturbing wildlife. This was not the easiest thing to agree to as Conachair in particular would need a lot of gardening if it was to be climbed. But Dave's visit cleared the air and afterwards we set about quizzing Pete and Ian on their previous three weeks on the island.

Pete Whillance was and was not what I had expected. A gaunt, almost haggard face seemed to indicate a dour and worried man. True, Pete puts himself under a lot of pressure, both in his academic work (he was completing his college thesis at the time) and in his climbing, where he has produced hundreds of new routes of the highest quality, mainly in the Lakes and Scotland. He can also be taciturn and slightly remote. But there was an immediate warmth and humanity in Pete that I quickly responded to; a wry sense of humour and above all an incredible conscientiousness in fulfilling everything he had set out to achieve. His partner, Ian McMullan, was also a fine climber in his own right, if more extrovert and laid back. It was obvious that they made up a formidable partnership.

Our first full day on St Kilda dawned bright but with the strong winds that were to be with us almost constantly for the next three weeks. The first job was to get the inflatables unpacked and, while Paddy organised their inflating, I reflected that, if past experience had taught me anything, what was coming next would not be very enjoyable. I had acquired, from Javlin, a Sheffield firm that specialised in sailing and climbing clothes, three snappy new wetsuits for Chris, Brian and myself. Whereas they looked as though they had just auditioned for bit parts in a James Bond movie, I looked like a cross between pop star Gary Glitter and a beached whale. Hot and uncomfortable, I gingerly eased myself into the bows of the inflatable, and prepared for another watery ordeal. We chugged off to test the engine, gradually increasing speed. I was amazed how hard the water felt as we smashed over the waves. It was exhilarating and not as unpleasant as I had feared. But we were quickly soaked and as we hadn't got a waterproof housing for the video camera I realised that any filming from boats had to be done in calm conditions.

Once both boats were declared seaworthy we decided to go round to look at Conachair. Conachair is actually the name of the highest hill on Hirta but its north side falls steeply into the sea in a complex series of cliffs. It is a debatable point which is the highest sea-cliff in Britain or Europe, with several contenders for the title. The Kame of Foula is one, as is Slieve League in Ireland, which is a full 600 metres high. But many of the really big cliffs are of no interest to the climber, whereas Conachair at its steepest point most definitely is. It is a straight 300 metres of vertical or overhanging granite with only a slight easing in its middle section.

On our first approach, we left the shelter of Village Bay and turned the first headland round what I always thought of as 'the other hill'. This is Oiseval, at 300 metres with its own set of impressive but smaller cliffs. We ploughed steadily along the coastline, each view bigger, more spectacular and more oppressive than the one before. Great buttresses of grey and orange granite soared upwards, choked with vegetation and streaked with water courses. Fulmars, thousands and thousands of them, wheeled and circled. In the vast surroundings they seemed more like flocks of starlings and it was hard to appreciate their size. At the foot of the cliffs the sea surged, sucked and smacked the rocks, plumes of spray shot high in the air, foam cascaded out of inlets and boiled over hidden reefs.

Many of the cliffs give out into huge hanging grass fields, or are obviously too loose to climb. Much of the north-facing rock is permanently wet. Seaward access to the base of the cliffs seemed suicidal. We rounded the next headland impressed but not inspired. Then Conachair itself loomed into sight.

Its great brooding bulk bears a strange resemblance to the North Face of the Eiger, for it is a huge amphitheatre, wide at the base and tapering towards the top. Before I left home I had rung Joe Brown to ask about it. He described the bottom third as being like a giant version of Carreg Hylldrem, a violently overhanging roadside crag in North Wales. Above that, he said, was a great sheet of blank slabs topped by a final 120 metres of vertical cracks and corners like the East Buttress of Cloggy. It was a remarkably accurate description but did little justice to the awesome grandeur of the place.

Paddy nosed the inflatable towards the base of the cliff and, in its dank shadows, we craned our necks skywards at the reeling chaos of overlapping rock suspended above us. Howard and Steve claimed that they could spot a line that took the lower wall direct to the great series of cracks and corners. It looked horrendous to me and, as it was dripping wet, I couldn't see how they could hope to climb it without a lot of artificial aid. Further right, however, the angle appeared to lean back and an easy angled ramp came down to the sea, giving an obvious landing. Pete and Ian had previously got ashore from an army inflatable, inspected the base of the cliff here and chosen a line leading up and through the first band of overhangs. It too looked improbable, but mine was certainly not to reason why, for I knew that even at my fittest I would stand absolutely no chance of climbing it. This was a view shared, if not actually admitted to, by most of us, even Chris, who declared quite forcefully that his role on Conachair would be confined to still photographer and reporter.

Whatever happened in the following three weeks an ascent of Conachair would not happen quickly, for the whole of the two prospective lines chosen by Pete and Ian and Howard and Steve would need a vast amount of gardening before they would have any chance of success. Meanwhile there were other crags to visit and the island of Hirta to explore. A slightly pensive team returned to Village Bay. At least, I thought as the jetty drew nearer, I hadn't felt sick in the inflatable.

During the first week everyone rushed round Hirta grabbing the obvious minor plums. Whereas the granite of Conachair was either brittle and featureless or compact and overhanging with many blind cracks, most of the other crags were made of sound grey gabbro giving fine climbing, almost all in the Hard Very Severe to Extreme bracket. Steve and Howard probably did the hardest single pitch: a huge roof on the West Face of Mullach Bi, but Mike and Marjorie were also producing new routes every day and Chris and Brian were equally enthusiastic. Paddy and I did one or two easy routes but I was climbing badly. I had done little if any rock climbing in the past year and, since my return from K2, had become horribly overweight and unfit. I was psychologically unprepared for serious sea-cliff climbing and still found it very hard not to dwell on the disasters of the previous summer.

One day, in blustery gale-force wind and rain, I walked up Oiseval on my own. The weather cleared, as it often did on St Kilda, with extraordinary rapidity. A large, two-masted yacht, which had taken shelter from the high winds, was berthed in Village Bay. As I reached the summit, sunlight hit the sea around it turning the whole bay into a golden, shimmering mirror. I sat down and, for the first time since leaving K2 Base Camp, I wept for my friend Al Rouse without inhibition. A total sorrow overwhelmed me, that he was not here to see this, that I would never share with him our very similar sense of humour, would never listen to another improbable Rouse story. All that had happened in the last year, the theories and recriminations about K2, the work on book and film, had happened without Al's knowledge or influence. Gradually a feeling of acceptance replaced the grief. Al, frozen to death at 8000 metres on K2, was no longer part of my life. Buried deep under the snows of Camp 4, for him it had all finished a year ago. There was simply no point in wishing it was not so. I gazed out at the grey Atlantic, storm-tossed in the late afternoon sun. That would be there for ever and a day. Whether Al had lived to be seventy instead of thirty-five, whether I died tomorrow or staggered on to be a hundred, it was all pretty insignificant anyway.

Every night some of us would wend down to the ugly army prefabs and into their bar, the Puff Inn, a large, sparsely furnished room with a pool table and dart board, patronised by squaddies and the odd civilian contractors. Apart from Marjorie it was exclusively a male society. The army presence was to man a missile-tracking station on the top of Mullach Bi that monitored rocket firings from the army base on Benbecula. I wondered how much other monitoring went on, for the sea around St Kilda was alive with shipping, in which the Russian fishing fleet was prominent. Doubtless submarine activity was equally active. Whatever their duties the platoon stationed on St Kilda seemed bored stiff at their posting and hardly any of them stirred out of the army quarters. It was ironic that with so many naturalists, ornithologists, scuba divers, climbers and walkers desperate for the chance of

The new relaxed Bonington.

visiting St Kilda, the thirty or so men who actually lived there were nearly all as equally desperate for the chance to leave.

One wet and gale-ridden day Chris went for a long run up Oesival, over to Conachair and then round the whole island. He returned glowing with good health. 'You know,' he enthused over a cup of tea, 'from the top of Conachair a stray shaft of sunlight lit up Village Bay and just for a moment I thought, gosh, even the army barracks looked good in this light.'

There was a stunned silence. Both the warden, Dave Miller and the Commanding Officer happened to be visiting. 'I shall pretend I didn't hear that,' said Dave, rather primly.

'You two-faced git, Bonington,' I heard Ian McMullan mutter into his mug.

'Well I think it sucks,' said the CO with finality.

'Er, well, yes, of course it is pretty grim,' Chris conceded lamely, removing his foot from his mouth.

Chris maintained his fine form throughout the whole three weeks (with one famous exception that was to come). I have always found it very easy to work with him for he has a real professional understanding of what is required. But there is no doubt that our own insecurities rub off on each other. Chris now grins and bears it when I tactlessly recount Bonington stories, though I am sure he wishes I wouldn't. For his part Chris still finds it hard to resist the temptation to tell me how to do my job. The biggest difference in Chris on this trip was one that many people have noticed. Since his own ascent of Everest in 1985, he has become fulfilled and relaxed. The 'edge' of always having to compete, to be in control and in the end to dominate, seems to have been blunted. Now he is climbing for pleasure and rock climbing better than ever. His greatest strength has always been his eternal enthusiasm and optimism about climbing and I have always admired (and been influenced by) his ability to snatch climbs, however insignificant, at the slightest opportunity. He is of course interested in the mechanics of power and aware of his own clout within the climbing world. Now, as President of the British Mountaineering Council, Chris has accepted the role of conciliator, arbiter and negotiator which ten years ago I am sure he would have found impossible. The new, relaxed Chris is certainly far more fun to be with and on St Kilda he was so laid back as to be able to have the odd day festering, reading and chatting without the old neurotic drive I had seen on Kongur to justify every minute of each waking hour with work of some kind.

The wild days seemed to become more frequent as the trip slipped over the halfway mark. We had made only one serious foray on to Conachair, when a gale warning precipitated the undignified retreat described at the opening of this chapter.

But now, with only a week or so left, we were still a long way from a first ascent. Pete and Ian were the only pair still interested in Conachair and had left abseil ropes down its entire length. They spent hours each day, whatever the weather, cleaning and scraping a line out of the steep, vegetated upper section of the cliff, and then trying to find a feasible way through the first compact and overlapping boiler plate walls. The rest of us climbed when we could and hoped that there would still be time for our other as yet unfulfilled objectives. These included visiting the Island of Soay which, rumour had it, could give the best climbs of all, and an ascent of Stac Biorach between Hirta and Soay which had often been climbed by the original islanders.

One wet day I visited the rather sad remnants of St Kilda's past.

These consisted of the little museum, the chapel and the school. The museum told the story simply and evocatively. The St Kildans had been a self-sufficient society almost entirely cut off from mainland Scotland until the mid-eighteenth century. They lived a life virtually unchanged since the Middle Ages, farming and relying largely on the flesh and eggs of sea-birds for food. They had become incredibly adept at scaling and descending cliffs to trap the birds and collect their eggs and used handwoven ropes for primitive lowering and 'top roping' manoeuvres. The St Kildans had adapted to their environment, with ankles half as wide again as a normal person and toes set further apart and almost prehensile. Life on the islands must, to the Victorian tourists who 'discovered' them, have seemed harsh, but something approaching an innocent idyll, if somewhat smelly. But as communications improved, and the islanders became aware of the outside world, their numbers dwindled. Eventually there were not enough able-bodied men to support an increasingly elderly and infirm population and on 29th August 1930, the last thirty-six islanders were evacuated to the Scottish mainland by the British navy.

In the schoolroom a slate still had an alphabet written in childish letters. B was for Bird and E for Egg, I was amused to read. The old schoolbooks still lay on the shelves, the last register recorded the few children who attended. The chapel was a bleak room with a disproportionately large pulpit from which the Wee Free Presbyterian minister would harangue his congregation on the dangers of trying to enjoy their harsh existence. This apparently happened three times every Sunday.

There is no doubt at all, Curran, I told myself as I walked back through the whipping wind and rain to the cottages, that compared to the vast majority of the human race past and present, you have had a bloody brilliant life, so don't ever complain. I don't believe in reincarnation, so the possibility of returning as a Balti porter, a slug or a zebra holds no fear for me. However, I was glad I hadn't been a St Kildan.

15

THE EDGE OF THE WORLD

WITH ONLY a week left before the return of the *Charna*, anxiety was mounting. The route on Conachair was more or less prepared, with bolts placed at stances and vast amounts of vegetation removed. It had been a job akin to painting the Forth Bridge or weeding the Hanging Gardens of Babylon. But would there be any chance of actually climbing it?

One day we decided to drop Pete and Ian off at the foot of the crag to complete their field study while the rest of us went for a trip round Soay. I had improvised a cover for the video camera made from a heavy-duty polythene water-carrier and a mass of camera tape. In reasonable seas I could film without the camera getting soaked in salt water. Filming them jumping ashore in the heavy swell at the foot of Conachair was a must, for it looked as dangerous as it undoubtedly was. We set off once again in both inflatables.

Unfortunately I had got comprehensively plastered in the Puff Inn with Paddy the previous evening. He showed no ill effects whatever but I was horribly hung over. Even the trip round to the crag, which I normally enjoyed, was grim and at the base of Conachair, while Pete and Ian prepared to jump out of the other inflatable, we circled round with our outboard engine throttled back. Vile fumes filled the air and, losing way, the boat pitched and rolled in the swell. Oh, God, here we go again. Just as the others made their final approach to the point where they would leap on to the sea-washed ledges I was evilly sick. This time Chris was understandably less than sympathetic. 'Film, you bastard, film!' he ordered in his best Captain Bligh voice. Pete and Ian jumped ashore and by a miracle I had the camera going and, though I was actually being sick at the time, managed to grab the crucial seconds. I was amused later on to see the shot fronting *News at Ten*, and wondered if the editors at ITN realised that the cameraman was barely conscious at the time.

At last we got under way again and headed off to Soay. The swell built up as we headed out to sea and I have never felt so awful. Chris, meanwhile, was waxing eloquent at the sight of the huge gabbro cliffs on the seaward side of Soay and bitterly regretting that we couldn't land. I wanted to die as soon as possible but the trip round the island was interminable. We completed the full circuit with a dramatic pass under Stac Biorach. Hundreds of seals toppled off rocks they had been basking on and swam effortlessly round us. Now, instead of going straight back to Village Bay, we explored the coastline around Glen Bay, with its huge caves and the famous Tunnel or Geo nalh-Airde. The inflatables nosed into its dark green depths, water slid, gurgled and slurped inside and I wanted to jump in and drown.

Eventually we turned for home. Racked by empty spasms of puking, and shivering violently, I started developing migraine symptoms and by the time we reached the jetty I could hardly see. As we docked Chris dropped an Olympus into the water. Retribution, I thought uncharitably.

Undeterred, Chris spent most of the rest of the day scheming ways and means to get to climb on Soay. He had been to Everest with the Norwegian shipping magnate and millionaire Arne Naess who was a keen amateur climber. 'I wonder,' he mused, 'if Arne would hire a helicopter to drop us off on Soay for four or five days then come and pick us up; that would be the way to do it, without that bloody awful sea voyage.' Arne Naess had recently married Diana Ross, the pop megastar, and for a brief moment I had a wonderful vision of her in a tight sequined evening dress with long white gloves up to her elbows singing 'Baby Love' in the Puff Inn before a small collection of incredulous drunken squaddies. About as likely to happen, I thought, as Chris arriving on Soay on a Sea King helicopter.

With only three full days to go the weather had clamped in completely, but there was a vaguely better forecast for the last day but one. This had to be it, in any case, for we had a mass of clearing up and packing to do on the last day. We all resolved to get up at five a.m. and go to the foot of Conachair. While Pete and Ian climbed the first pitches I was to film from the ramp at the bottom, then return and go round to the top of Conachair and abseil down its easy north-western flank to a superb vantage-point just above the halfway point. Finally, we hoped, I could film down the final corner crack as they completed the climb. It was a realistic, though ambitious plan and clearly demanded good weather, good timing and a lot of effort from every one (particularly, of course, Pete and Ian).

After a broken, tension-filled night, we awoke to the shrill of the alarm clock and the drumming of rain on the cottage roof. Bloody hell. An hour later it had eased off and we decided at least to go and have a look. As soon as we left Village Bay we were plunging and rising on the biggest swell yet. When Conachair came into view one look was enough. Waves crashed over the landing area and wet, weeping streaks of seepage stained the lower walls. 'That's it then – no chance.' Flat anticlimax as we turned and battled back to a hot shower and a second breakfast.

I felt desperately sorry for Pete in particular, for he was obsessed with the need to justify the whole expedition with this, the big one. It didn't matter how many other routes we had done, or how hard, if Conachair remained unclimbed. I wondered if there was even the slightest chance of having one last attempt tomorrow if we got everything packed up today. As I finished my shower and walked up to the cottages I noticed Pete and Ian, carrying rucksacks, hot-footing it up the steep hillside behind the cottages en route to Conachair. What was happening?

Chris was getting ready. 'They've changed their minds – they're going to abseil in and try it anyway.' Quickly we hatched another plan. Chris would abseil down as well with the video camera and get what we could from the bottom. Brian would then bring the camera up to me, in position at the halfway point. After that we'd just have to see.

At the very top of the cliff a short scramble down an unnervingly loose and muddy slope led to a large cleit perched on a big grassy ledge. Cleits are stone beehive-shaped structures in which the St Kildans used to hang their birds to dry. This one was actually being used to anchor the fixed ropes that led down steep, wet grass terraces to the halfway point. The others had already descended. I always find fixed ropes far easier to deal with on my own, without the distractions of others. I half abseiled, half walked to the point where I could peer over and into the huge concave face and lashed myself to every available belay. There was no sign of anyone climbing. Far below thunderous waves crashed into the base of the cliff. The air was full of fulmars circling, whirling and plunging into the void. If I looked at them for too long I felt quite queasy.

On the rock promontory at the foot of the crag, Chris had set himself up to watch, comment and film Pete and Ian. It was nearly midday before they got started, jumaring up the first steep slabs they had climbed on the early visit. Then Pete set off on the first of the key pitches, a great diagonal rising traverse that was to break through the first band of overhangs. Later Chris described it as some of the most impressive rock climbing he had ever seen. It was steep, delicate, devious and appallingly protected. As Pete inched further and further from the belay he risked a bigger and bigger fall into space. His ropes were dragging badly and he had to keep pulling enough slack out to make the next moves. At one point, just above a very poor protection peg, Pete took three short falls, stopping himself each time by grabbing the sling attached to the peg. Finally he managed to teeter up the bulging wall above and, by now really out on a limb, completed another ten metres of desperate, unprotected climbing to the bolt stance he had previously prepared.

Ian was now faced with the classic seconding nightmare: a traverse out of sight and earshot of the leader with the hard moves coming just after unclipping the protection, and the prospect of ending up in space if he fell. Later, Chris's video of Ian's performance was about as gripping to watch as it must have been for Ian to climb. Halfway across he all but blew it and Chris's vivid commentary made it even more compelling viewing.

While all the drama was being enacted, I was sitting half asleep on my perch, occasionally leaning out on the belays to see if anyone was visible. At last I caught a glimpse of Pete's magenta jacket and, as he disappeared under an overhang, I heard a shout and the faint jangle of gear. He reappeared a few minutes later, climbing with studied ease towards a belay in the middle of what we called the Pink Walls. Brian suddenly popped up on the fixed ropes below me with the camera, which he had hauled up from Chris below, and I was roused into action. Chris arrived later and, perched on a grass ledge with deep blue sea and Boreray and the Stacks framed behind him, did a superb piece to camera that ITN used to introduce their extensive news feature.

Ian and Pete were both sorting out their belay stance so to save power I switched off the camera until the next bit of action. Suddenly, unexpectedly, Ian was off! – a little marionette figure tumbling into space. Pete held him after only a few feet and Ian, shaken, regained the stance.

Inevitably came the question, 'Did you film that?'

'Did I, buggery.'

There had been a light shower and the following pitch, a long groove, was wet. Pete seemed to have taken over all the leading. He has the mark of the great climber in that he makes everything look easy. Despite having stopped smoking for five years I can still be tempted by Pete's nonchalant ability to light up in the middle of a pitch: both hands off the rock and then in the most unlikely positions, cigarette in mouth, he weighs up the holds ahead. When he moves it is with decision and a kind of economical agility. At the top of the groove he seemed to have reached easier ground and all that remained were the upper 120 metres of vertical corner cracks, supposedly much easier. It was six p.m. and already the mid-September light was fading. The film team decided to go to the top of the crag, though how I was supposed to work in pitch darkness I wasn't sure. Halfway up the fixed ropes I filmed the sun sinking into the sea behind Soay. Great rays of light were flung across the cloudy skies before the world went grey and dusk was upon us.

We all gathered at the cleit in the last flickers of daylight and cautiously descended to the point where we could look straight over the final corner. Even in near total darkness it was a horrifying drop. Far, far below I could just distinguish white surf at the base of the crag. It was the stuff of nightmares and even with the security of the fixed rope it was hard not to give way to utter panic. There was no sight nor sound of Pete and Ian and no answer to our calls.

At last, peering down we saw something move; a faint red glow appeared from under an overhang. Pete, with cigarette burning, was peering up at the final corner. It was an incredibly impressive sight as the pinprick of red advanced towards us. We shone torches down the corner, trying to light up the rock and not dazzle Pete, who as he got nearer, told us that he had run out of nuts and Friends to protect himself. He was now about fifteen metres above his last runner. Through the viewfinder I could just distinguish a shadowy image and decided that nothing would be lost by running the camera. As Pete neared the top he was caught in the torchbeams like a wartime bomber in searchlights. Only another few metres to go and I could see him quite clearly in the viewfinder. Shouted contradictory advice was being given, now he was almost up. 'Quick, grab the fixed rope!'

'No way – I've done the whole thing free, I'm not cheating the last move.' Bridging across the top of the corner with 300 metres of space below him, Pete made the final mantelshelf to a great chorus of congratulations from all of us. Forgetting I was filming, I yelled, 'Fan-bloody-tastic!' before realising the camera was running. Once again ITN kept it in. Joyfully, cluttered with gear, we scrambled back to the cleit. Pete brought Ian up quickly and I got them both, normally taciturn, to give voluble first impressions of their route. Both agreed it was the hardest thing they'd ever done.

Later, over a pint in the Puff Inn Pete and Ian unwound and gave their verdict on the route. They graded the climb E6. In Britain E, or Extreme, grades go from 1 to, at present, 7 or 8. My upper limit is to very occasionally second E1 or E2. E6 is unimaginably more serious. The technical grades of each pitch were 5b, 5c, 6b, 5b, 6a, 5c, 5b, 5c. I have occasionally been dragged up 5c on gritstone on the end of a tight rope. Leading 6b in the situations on Conachair was almost a different sport.

Dave Miller had been doing his homework. 'Did you realise,' he said, 'that cleit we used as an anchor is known as the Cleit on the Edge of the World?'

Immediately, an amazingly impressive climb had acquired a name to match.

The *Charna* returned for us a day early because of gale warnings, and the return was really rough. I stayed below in my sleeping-bag for the entire voyage. Before long Chris came below and this time even he looked unhappy. 'Oh, God we've got another twenty hours of this,' he groaned as he returned from one of many visits to the lavatory.

'I don't suppose you feel like taking a last photo of the islands, then?' I asked him callously.

'Point taken,' he muttered.

It took twenty-eight hours before we saw the welcome lights of Oban the following evening. This, I thought, really is my last boat trip. We tied up against the quayside and the throb of the engines ceased. 'I quite fancy going to Foula one day,' I heard myself saying, to my amazement. With this bit of breathtaking self-delusion another adventure was over.

16

TO BE
CONTINUED . . .

IN 1988 I went to Everest at last. A large team, led by Brummie Stokes and including Joe and Mo, went for the second time to attempt the long unclimbed North-East Ridge, where Joe Tasker and Pete Boardman had disappeared in 1982. I was to film for HTV, but I fell ill almost at the beginning of the expedition and never got on to the mountain. It was still a great experience to film in Tibet, to see Lhasa, and visit the Rongbuk Monastery.

We arrived at Base Camp in thick cloud. Joe had said that he wanted to see my face when I saw Everest for the first time. 'You're absolutely bound to cry, and I want to take a photo of you.' But there was no sight of the mountain and indeed not much clue that we were in the Himalaya at all. The Rongbuk valley is more Scottish in scale than Himalayan and the idea that we were now less than fifteen miles from the highest point on earth was difficult to accept.

Feeling lightheaded and breathless I slept badly and woke very early. I peered through the tent flap and saw a glimpse of something white through breaking cloud. I got up and in the quiet campsite stood in awe as the famous view slowly appeared. There were the First and Second Steps, the Great Couloir, the Pinnacles, Changtse, the Yellow Band and of course the summit itself.

No tears came to my eyes, I was pleased to tell Joe later. Instead a curious feeling of being very slightly let down. Just for once it was exactly as I had imagined it. My first, and I have to say enduring impression was that it didn't look big enough. Very occasionally in shifting cloud the scale of Everest was revealed but to me its proportions fitted the landscape so well it didn't seem much bigger than Snowdon seen from Capel Curig. Certainly compared with the classic view of K2 from Concordia, Everest didn't look terribly impressive.

But what it lacked in spectacle it certainly made up for in sheer atmosphere for we were camped on the same site as the pre-war Everest expeditions. Above was the mound of moraine on which had stood the cairn in memory of Mallory and Irvine and the Sherpas who had died on Everest up to 1924.

Our expedition was a partial success. Harry Taylor and Russell Bryce, two extremely fit and determined climbers, succeeded in getting across the famous Pinnacles and in doing so completed the unclimbed section of the Ridge. But heavy snow stopped them making a summit bid and they had to make a very committing and dangerous descent to the North Col and down to Advance Base. It was a brilliant effort but a slightly frustrating end to the expedition.

Overshadowing Everest was the desperate realisation that Mo, brilliant, irrepressible Mo Anthoine, was dying. In January 1988 I had first heard that Mo had a brain tumour and would be operated on immediately. Distraught and fighting back tears, I rang up to wish him well. As usual Mo was his incorrigible self. 'Village idiot speaking,' he greeted me. 'Don't worry, there's only three things that can happen. Either they'll remove it and I'll be okay, or they'll turn me into a vegetable.' He paused.

'What's the third?'

'If they bugger it up completely I'll have to get a job at Plas y Brenin as an instructor.'

The operation appeared to be a complete success and, undeterred, Mo had gone to Everest. With most of the equipment he got to Base Camp three weeks before the main party and greeted us with delight when we at last caught him up. He looked thin and drawn, though his humour was undiminished and as macabre as ever. 'If I get really ill, Jim, I want you to film me as I throw myself down the Kangshung Face, doused in paraffin and burning like a Viking warrior.'

Despite performing well (and, incidentally, doing the lion's share of the filming himself when I was ill) Mo's health had deteriorated by the end of the year. He bore his illness, and another operation, with a courage and humour that was moving beyond words. Many visitors came away from the house still laughing through the tears. Even near the end a small part of me hoped, irrationally, that Mo could somehow manage to find a way out and he would turn up laughing in the pub, but it was not to be.

Sometimes on a climb or at a party a fragment of one of Mo's great stories or a famous one-liner will resurface and heart-warming bittersweet memories are revived. Of the many wonderful days I spent climbing with him, one of the best was one of the last, when Mo and

Joe came down on a rare visit to Bristol to do the Bonington Cheddar Gorge classic, Coronation Street. I'd climbed it once myself in the seventies and vowed then once was enough. But I could not resist an outing with Mo and Joe. We met, of course, in a pub.

'It's Jibble,' Mo greeted me. The name originated from Mo's first visit to Bristol and the discovery that Bristolians add a final l to words ending in a vowel, the classic sentence being 'The primal donnal sang an arial at the operal.' It didn't take Mo long to turn me into Jiml, which on his meeting Gemma and Becky for the first time became Jibble and the Giblets. The name stuck. Standing in the car park underneath the great High Rock craning up at the cracks and grooves of Coronation Street high above, all the good reasons for chickening out came rushing back. Joe always has that effect on me, but he and Mo insisted that I roped up and there was no escape.

It was as hard as I remembered but between fits of laughter at Mo's eternal piss-taking I did manage to climb it marginally better than on the first occasion. 'You must have been absolutely bloody useless the last time then,' was Joe's accurate assessment when I stupidly told him this. Mo insisted on going second which left me at the end of the rope on the horrible traverse of the famous Shield. This is actually technically the easiest pitch on the climb but sensational and unnerving to second. You almost have to hand traverse a horizontal break, removing the runners before doing the hard moves, to end up with a great lurch on big jugs round a corner to a hanging stance below the long crux pitch up a big right-angled groove. Joe led it in about five minutes, saying it was easy. Mo followed him climbing as well as I've ever seen him and I was left dangling alone above a hundred metres of space, waiting to unclip from the belays and start the pitch. At last Joe's helmeted head peered down the corner. 'Okay, Jim, how much do you want to weigh? Ha, ha, ha.'

'About two stone less than I do now. Is there petrol in the winch?'

The rope went drum tight. Featherlight, I bridged swiftly up the crack, occasionally giving the bigger holds a passing caress as Joe pulled in the ropes. I jammed up the final crack above an overhang with all the space in the Cheddar Gorge snapping at my feet, and joined Joe and Mo on the tiny ledge overlooking the huge drop. Safely clipped in I preferred to look closely at the grey, lichenous rock in front of me.

'What are you staring at?' enquired Joe.

'Nothing, I just don't want to look the other way,' I replied feebly.

Joe got the giggles at this and set off on the last pitch. I couldn't help grinning to myself. It was ten years since I had been there, bedraggled and terrified on the same stance in the dusk and rain. Now, still frightened, I watched Joe scamper up the last few feet. Mo, next to me, was obviously quite impressed. 'Don't jump off while I'm climbing, will you?' he requested. The idea made me feel quite faint and I clutched the rock with clammy hands.

At the top we coiled the ropes and walked down the rough path back to the car. The sun was setting over the Bristol Channel and we were going out for a huge meal in a Greek restaurant in Bristol. It is almost impossible to come to terms with the fact that Mo will no longer be one of the party. But as long as there are people who knew him, Mo will live on in a rich kaleidoscope of images, words and events. In fifty hectic years Mo lived a complete life that few people could attain in one hundred.

In March 1989 I celebrated my thirtieth 'birthday' as a climber. With Steve Durkin I drove down to Sussex and on a wretched, misty, rainy day returned to Chiddingly Wood Rocks. In the new guidebook to south-east England it is now referred to as Chiddinglye Wood, which I found strangely disturbing. We took great delight in being forty-six-year-old trespassers. In pouring rain we soloed the first route we ever climbed and then failed to top rope the one next to it. We walked down the valley to Great-upon-Little, the strange boulder perched on a tiny plinth. In the valley the rhododendrons had been cleared and a primitive showjumping course with ugly petrol drums and crude fences had been laid out. There was still no sign of the ghostly canine apparition, Gytrack, but I imagine he must have given up in disgust for there is now nothing much left to haunt. However, the hermit's cave was still the same, the strange tree roots embedded in the dark recesses that a sixteen-year-old Mike Watkins had been convinced was a snake. We returned to the car and I was suddenly once more aware of the evocative smell of sandstone and leaf mould. A pity we didn't bring a hemp rope for the day.

We left and drove over to High Rocks Hotel for a nostalgic pint. Then, late in the afternoon, the rain stopped and we went to a dark and sodden Harrisons Rocks. There was just time to top rope a few old classics. Despite the evil, slimy sandstone and a twenty-year (at least) absence, I remembered how to do Hell Wall and Moonlight Arête. In the dusk, walking back to the car, the years compressed and memories flooded back. 'I think we definitely ought to come back for our fiftieth anniversary, Steve, even if we need wheelchairs and nurses to get us here!'

1990 started well, with the construction of my own climbing wall in the ginnel beside my house. On winter evenings I could train by simply stepping outside the front door, struggling for a few minutes on the prefabricated holds bolted to the brickwork, and coming in to warm my aching hands in front of the sitting-room fire. The year really took off at Easter with a great holiday in Morocco, first snow-plodding in the High Atlas Mountains, then bouldering and struggling on single pitch rock routes in the awe-inspiring Todra Gorge on the edge of the Sahara Desert. Tony Iveson, my climbing partner from Bristol, shared both the holiday and my new-found enthusiasm. In an unusually fine English spring I seemed to be climbing almost every evening.

In Sheffield Mike Richardson was climbing better than ever. Mike, in his mid-forties, has had a dramatic reawakening of his enthusiasm for rock climbing. For many years a keen club cyclist, he was as happy to pedal through Derbyshire as climb in it. Then in 1985 he started getting it together again. Mike is a big man, immensely strong and technically very good. We are both convinced that we are approaching senility and our outings to Derbyshire, particularly when Paul Nunn is around, are like scenes from the TV comedy, *Last of the Summer Wine*. Young climbers were often bemused at the apparition of three enormous old men, still climbing at a more than respectable standard.

Another Sheffield neighbour, Joe Simpson, was well on the way to recapturing the high standard he had reached before his horrific accident in Peru in 1985. Both of us were labouring with unfinished books and the gritstone edges were constantly tempting us away from them.

One red-letter day with Joe and Mike was long overdue. Joe led Mike and me (at last at the age of forty-seven) up Cenotaph Corner. Its reputation intimidated me and wasn't helped by the leader in front of us who took a long and unexpected fall before he got up. I finally hauled myself over the top, dry-mouthed and barely able to speak to my trusty belayers. But that evening in Llanberis I sat in the kitchen of another climber called Joe. I offered him belated congratulations on one of the greatest climbs in Wales. The Baron Brown handed me a glass of wine and laughed at my pomposity. He then said something very rude to me which Joe Simpson, Mike and I laughed at until our sides ached. Sadly it's unprintable.

In August, to my delight, I was invited, out of the blue, to be cameraman in a project masterminded by Richard Else, a producer at BBC North-East in Newcastle. This would eventually be a six-part series on the history of mountaineering and the programme I was to shoot would be discussing Himalayan climbing underneath the

Charlie Houston's stories of Tilman and Odell on Nanda Devi sounded as though they happened yesterday.

colossal Diamir Face of Nanga Parbat with three great veterans, Chris Bonington, Charlie Houston and Sigi Hupfauer.

I was eager to meet Charlie. He had sent me a very kind letter after the publication of my K2 book; a greater testimonial could not be imagined. In it he had told me how the Art Gilkey disaster on K2 in 1953 had effectively ended his active climbing career. For years afterwards he had suffered major depressions on the anniversary of Gilkey's death, 10th August. By coincidence this was the day that 'Mrufka' Wolf died on the descent of the Abruzzi Ridge in 1986 and, in all probability, the day Al Rouse also died at Camp 4 on the Shoulder of K2. The letter had moved me deeply as I also find the days surrounding the anniversary a distressing time. Perhaps by going back to Pakistan with Charlie, if not to K2 itself, but to a mountain with its own long history of triumph and tragedy I, or we, might be able to make some kind of sense of it all. In any case I felt I could now revisit the area, and it might rekindle my enthusiasm for the whole Karakoram which has meant so much to me over the years.

Sigi Hupfauer from Ulm in Germany is not well known in Britain, yet his track record is quite incredible: eight of the fourteen 8000-metre peaks (including Everest and Nanga Parbat), ten of the 7000ers and forty-two 6000ers! I had met him once before at K2 Base Camp in 1986 when he had walked across from the nearby Broad Peak Base Camp with his wife in the forlorn hope that he could be of any help in coping with the horrifying events that were occurring high on the Abruzzi Ridge. I had been struck by his genuine concern and appreciation of the situation. I looked forward to meeting him properly. His vast experience and knowledge would add a vital perspective to our film, for Nanga Parbat has always been known as a German mountain.

The walk up the Diamir valley is short but beautiful, with Nanga Parbat and the Monzino Ridge framed at its head. Charlie Houston's stories of Tilman and Odell on Nanda Devi sounded as though they happened only yesterday. Frequently he would look around in wonder at the views and quote Odell who, after the Everest expedition of 1924 when Mallory and Irvine disappeared, had not returned to the Himalaya until 1936. Then, on the first day of the walk-in to Nanda Devi, Odell had suddenly flung his arms heavenwards and yelled at the top of his voice, 'God! It's just so good to be back!' Houston's strong voice would frequently reaffirm Odell's sentiments. Then he would add: 'I must have been crazy to come here, but it will be even harder to leave. If I make it to Base Camp, I sure won't make it back home again.' But, by pacing himself superbly Charlie would stroll into camp each afternoon smiling to himself and clearly enjoying every minute of this curious adventure.

Only Sigi had been here before and at each village little children would run to greet him shouting 'Sigi Zindabad! Sigi Zindabad!' (Long live Sigi!). He had brought small presents to give the kids – little paper windmills, pencils and paper. His generosity was both simple and practical. Every evening he dispensed medicine and advice to long queues of patients, who clamoured for pills of all sort for illnesses real and imaginary. I have rarely met such a kind-hearted man.

We were incredibly lucky with the weather and had breathtaking views every day. With Richard Else I felt a strongly supportive presence, as well as a very similar philosophy towards film-making. The only fly in the ointment was when we reached Base Camp, situated on what should have been an idyllic green pasture at the bottom of the Diamir Face. Our pleasure was turned to disgust, then anger, at the piles of odious and all-pervading rubbish abandoned by previous expeditions. Inside a sun-bleached frame tent were dozens of abandoned medical test tubes full of congealed blood. Half-empty tins of food and packages, polythene bags, human excrement and broken glass lay scattered over a huge area. No real attempt had been made to burn, bury or remove it. It was by far the worst mess I have ever seen in the mountains. The K2 and Everest Base Camps were nothing beside this, for it was so obviously avoidable. During our two-day stay we tried to clean up one small area and burnt twelve large plastic drums worth of rubbish in one afternoon. But we barely scratched the surface. With sadness Charlie quoted Oscar Wilde: 'Yet each man kills the thing he loves . . .'

Despite the filth, it was still an impressive place to sit and stare. Above us towered the Diamir Face, the Mummery Rib in the centre, a slim tapering buttress marking the imaginative line Mummery attempted in 1895 on what was almost the first real foray into the then unknown world of Himalayan climbing. To the left was the big buttress of the Kinshofer Route, first climbed in 1970 and more recently by Sigi in 1988. The Diamir Face was also the scene of an epic descent by Reinhold Messner and his brother Günther. Günther died almost within reach of safety in an avalanche in 1970. Messner returned and made a brilliant solo ascent of the Face in 1978. Between the eighty-three years separating Mummery's and Messner's efforts lay the almost complete story of Himalayan developments. The stupendous backdrop was the setting for Charlie, Sigi and Chris to spend a day reflecting on some of the major events of twentieth-century mountaineering. The filming went so smoothly I felt we were leading a charmed life.

With the film in the can I could relax, and spend the first long descent talking to Charlie Houston about K2 and his major role in two pre- and post-war expeditions. He recalled legendary figures like Bill House who led the first ascent of House's Chimney on the Abruzzi Ridge; Sherpa Kikuli who died in the attempted rescue of Dudley Wolfe in 1939; Art Gilkey in 1953 and Dee Molenaar, who can still make the delightful claim to be the highest practising artist in the world by painting a watercolour at over 7500 metres on the Abruzzi Ridge! Recounting these stories, and giving shrewd and highly informed opinions on many of the controversies surrounding K2 expeditions since Oscar Eckenstein's first expedition in 1902, Charlie's quietly but firmly stated arguments were deeply impressive and I felt a great wave of affection for the man who for so long had been a name on my bookshelves.

On this, my third filming venture with Chris, I was delighted that we had hit it off with no reservations. We had been forced, on humanitarian grounds, to share hotel rooms and a tent, as I have now come to realise to my horror that my own capacity for snoring is almost as bad as his. We were the social pariahs of the expedition and also, by a long way, the most chaotic, our tent a comfortable shambles of cameras, film, books, clothes and sleeping-bags.

We descended in great good humour towards the Karakoram Highway and the road home. On the last night, camping in a hot and dusty field, we went to bed early. Charlie stayed up for a while, sitting outside his tent and gazing into the brilliant starlit night illuminated above the black jagged ridges. I wondered what he was thinking as he absorbed the sights that had so dominated his life.

One week later I was at home in bed racked with a high temperature and diarrhoea. The phone rang. It was Richard. I prayed a silent prayer. 'I just wanted you to know that the film is almost perfect, just a few scratches at the end of the rolls and one shot over-exposed. But everything has worked exceptionally well and I'm delighted.' I heaved a sigh of relief and felt rather better immediately.

Another week later I received a letter from Charlie in Burlington, Vermont. 'Rumour has it you are in bed with Fever, but I'm not told whether this is a female, a ghost or a disease!'

INDEX

A Dream of White Horses, 139
A Great Effort, 39–40, 50, 73, 75
Allen, Marjorie, 161–2, 166
Allen, Nat, 129–30
Allt a' Mhuilinn, 76–7, 79, 81, 127
Alpine Club, 144
Alps, 28–30
Am Buchaille, 124
Ananea, 149, 154
Annapurna, South face, 36, 84, 138
Anthoine, Jackie, 47–8, 130–1, 139
Anthoine, Mo, 20, 37; friendship with
    Curran, 47–8, 50, 52; 1975 Trango
    Expedition, 51; 1876 Trango
    Expedition, 51–62, 64, 71, 96, 113,
    130–1, 139, 160, 176; illness, 177;
    1988 Everest Expedition, 176–7;
    climbing in Bristol, 178–9; death,
    179

Baltoro Cathedrals, 59
Baltoro Glacier, 52–3, 60
Barber, Henry, 118–19
Barker, Bill, 50
Barnaj II, 1977 Expedition, 63–72; Base
    Camp, 67, 69; Camp 1, 69–70; South
    Peak, 70; 1979 Expedition, 72, 81–2,
    143
Barnicott, Martin, 42
The Bat, 44, 78–82; The Hoodie
    Groove, 76–8; The Great Corner,
    78–80
The Bat and the Wicked (Robin Smith),
    73
Baxter-Jones, Roger, 74, 85
Ben Nevis, 28; The Bat, 73; Carn
    Dearg Buttress, 74–6, 79, 81, 120;
    North East Buttress, 127–8; Man
    Trap, 128; Centurion, 128
Bergercrack, 116
Biafo Glacier, 52, 64
Birtles, Geoff, 20, 56
Black Crag, 128
Boardman, Peter, 19, 20, 60, 85; 1981
    British Mount Kongus Expedition,
    87, 91, 93, 95, 99–109; death,
    110–11, 176
Bonington, Chris, 19, 21, 36, 39, 48,
    64; character, 84; 1981 British Mount
    Kongur Expedition, 83–4, 88, 91–6;

illness at Advance Base Camp, 98,
    101–2, 128–9, 139, 146, 149;
    Expedition to St Kilda, 159–69,
    170–5; 1985 Ascent of Everest, 168;
    Nanga Parbat, 180–4
Bonington, Wendy, 160
Bosigran, 116
Boulton, Chris, 37
Bow Shaped Slab, 131
Boyden, Steve, 159, 161, 165
Boysen, Maggie, 137
Boysen, Martin, 19; Curran's first
    meeting, 28, 36, 50–1; friendship
    with Curran, 54–5; 1976 Expedition
    to Trango, 59, 60
Braldu Gorge, 52
British Mount Kongur Expedition
    (1981), 83; first sight, 93; Base
    Camp, 94–6; Advance Base Camp,
    98; the Pimple, 97, 100; South Ridge
    ascent, 102–9; summit failure, 105;
    second successful summit bid, 106–8;
    Junction Peak ascent, 107; snow
    coffins, 108; summit celebrations,
    109
British Mountaineering Council, 118,
    139, 145, 168
Broad Peak, 138
Brown, Joe, 19, 28, 39, 50–1; Curran's
    first meeting, 55–6; recent
    expeditions, 56; 1976 Trango
    Expedition, 51, 60, 133, 134, 160,
    165; 1988 Everest Expedition, 176;
    climbing in Bristol, 178–9, 180
Bryce, Russell, 177
Burke, Mick, 71, 85
Burke, Phil, 115–16
Busk, Sir Douglas, 89

Calaghan, Barry, 44
Callejon, 149
Cape Wrath, 38
Capel Curig, 25, 31, 176
Carrington, Rab, 54, 55; The Bat,
    74–82, 85, 118
Carrington, Sue, 82, 137
Cartlege, Ian (Fox), 48
Cenotaph Corner, 180
Centurion, 76
Chair Ladder, 116, 134

Chameleon Films, 62, 68, 73, 110
Chamonix, 28–30, 160
Changabang, West Face, 60, 85
Cheddar Gorge, 38
Chiddingly Wood Rocks, 25–6, 67, 179
Choktoi, 1978 Expedition, 71
Citizen's Edge, 118
Clarke, Dr Charles, 91, 95, 102–3
cleits, 172
Climbers Club, 132, 134, 141, 161
Climbing competitions, 19
Clogwyn Du'r Arddu, 55, 78; White
  Slab, 128, 130, 165
Coffey, Maria, 130
Conachair, 160, 163–5, 167–8, 170–2,
  175
Congo Corner, 130
Cook, Dave, 118
Cordillera Apolobamba, 1985
  Expedition, 144, 146, 149
Cordillera Blanca, 143
Cordillera Real, 154–5
Coronation Street, 178–9
Craig Gogarth, 39, 139
Crew, Peter, 39
Crib Goch Ridge, 32, 42
Curran, Becky, 36, 115, 137, 160, 178
Curran, Gemma, 20, 35, 115, 137, 160,
  178
Curran, Jim, Nanga Parbat, 21–2;
  childhood, 23–6; early climbing,
  24–30; Cornwall, 24–5; North
  Wales, 25, 28; Chiddingly Wood,
  25–6; Harrisons Rocks, 25–6;
  Chamonix, 28–30; marriage to
  Alison, 31; Lliwedd, 31–4; birth of
  Gemma, Becky, moved to Bristol,
  35; break up of first marriage, 36;
  friendship with Nick Estcourt, 36–7;
  friendship with Paul Nunn, 37–8;
  friendship with Mo Anthoine, 47–8;
  1976 Trango Tower Expedition,
  51–61; friendship with Joe Brown,
  55–6; 1977 Expedition to Barnaj II,
  63–72; break-up of second marriage,
  83; death of mother, 83, 110; 1978
  Expedition to Choktoi, 71; 1979
  Expedition to Barnaj II, 72;
  friendship with Chris Bonington,
  83–4; British Mount Kongur

Expedition, 83–109; friendship with
  Alan Rouse, 85; Lundy, 112–14;
  Jersey, 115–18; girlfriend, Cass, 115,
  118; Radio Lollipop 100 sponsored
  climbs, 120–33; friendship with Don
  Whillans, 134–42; 1985 Expedition to
  Peru, 143–58; British Fullers
  Expedition to K2 (1986), 160; KS,
  Triumph and Tragedy published
  (1987), 160; trip to St Kilda, ITN
  climbing cameraman, 159–75; 1988
  Expedition to Everest, 176–7; BBC
  climbing cameraman on Nanga
  Parbat (1990), 180–4; film-making,
  Sheffield Polytechnic, 37; Tony
  Riley, 39; A Great Effort, 39–46;
  Trango, 52, 57–8, 62; filming on
  Barnaj, 65–8, 71; The Bat, 73–82;
  filming on Kongur, 84, 90, 102–10;
  K2, Triumph and Tragedy (film), 160;
  ITN cameraman on St Kilda, 159–75;
  BBC cameraman on Nanga Parbat,
  Base Camp, 180–4
Curran, Phil, 20, 24, 45

Dark, Bill, 115–16
Dearman, Bob, 42–3
Devenish, Robin, 24, 26–8
Devil's Kitchen, 40
Devil's Slide, 113
Diamir Face (Nanga Parbat), 181–3
Diamond Solitaire, 113
Diocese, 137
Doorpost, 132
Downes, Bob, 138
Durkin, Steve, 25, 31–4, 127, 179

Eckenstein, Oscar, 31, 183
Edwards, John Menlove, 39–40, 43,
  106
Eiger, The, 73, 85, 165
Else, Richard, 180, 182–4
Envers des Aiguilles, hut, 29
Estcourt, Nick, 20, 30; friendship with
  Curran, 36–7, 64
Everest, Mount, 23, 24, 84, 85; 1981
  West Ridge Expedition, 85; 1975
  South-West Ridge Expedition, 85;
  death of Boardman and Tasker,
  North-East Ridge, 110–11, 138, 168,

171; 1988 North-East Ridge attempt, 176–7; 1924 Expedition, 182

Fawcett, Lieutenant-Colonel P. N., 144
Fawcett, Ron, 113, 133
Film-making: Sheffield Polytechnic, 37; *A Great Effort*, 39–46; expedition filming versus dramatised documentary, 45; *Trango*, 57, 62; filming of Barnaj II, 63, 65–8; *Barnaj* shown at Motor Show, 71; *The Bat*, 73–81; editing *The Bat*, 82; premier, Kendal Mountaineering Film Festival (1981), 82; *Kongur* film proposal, 84, 88; filming on Kongur, 90–4; South Ridge Ascent, 102–9; editing *Kongur*, 110; *K2, Triumph and Tragedy* (1986), 160; ITN cameraman at St Kilda, 170–4; filming on Everest (1988), 176; BBC cameraman at Nanga Parbat (1990), 180–4
Foinavon, 127
Frêney Pillar, 73
Frost, Paddy, 159, 161, 164–5, 170

Gasherbrum I, 59, 60
Gasherbrum IV, 105
Géant, The, 29
Gez Gorge, 92
Ghosts Over England (R. Thurston Hopkins), 26
Gilgit, 22, 92
Gilkey, Art, 21, 181, 183
Grandes Jorasses, 29
Grépon, 29; Mer de Glace, 28; Knubel Crack, 29; South-West Ridge, 29

Hagshu Peak, 69
Hall, Brian, 74; *The Bat*, 75–82, 118; St Kilda, 164, 166, 172–3
Haramosh, 21
Hard Rock (Ken Wilson), 129
Hard Years, The (Joe Brown), 51
Harris, Al, 20, 37, 48; first meeting, 50; death, 110
Harrisons Rocks, 25–6, 179
Haston, Dougal, 73–4
Haszko, Richard, 115–16, 118
Henderson, Martin, 88, 91, 93
Herligkoffer, Dr Karl, 139

Heywood, Paul, 44
High magazine, 56, 156
Hopkinson, Pip, 112–14, 129–30
House, Bill, 183
Houston, Dr Charles, 21, 181–4
Howells, Malcolm, 1876 Trango Expedition, 56–7, 60, 71
Hunt, John, 24, 107, 146
Hupfauer, Sigi, 21, 181–3

Inca Trail, 158
In High Places (Dougal Haston), 73
Innocent, Carole, 88
Irvine, Andrew, 24, 177, 182
Iveson, Tony, 20, 180

Jannu, 74, 76, 85
Jardine, Matheson, 88, 90
Jersey, first visit, 115–18
Jewhurst, Allen, 62, 68

K2, 19, 21, 45, 53, 60, 62, 96, 111, 118, 138, 139; British Fullers Expedition (1986), 160, 162, 176; *K2, Triumph and Tragedy* (Jim Curran), book and film, 160, 181–2, 183
Kame of Foula, The, 164
Kangchenjunga, North Ridge, 85
Karakoram Highway, 21
Kendal Mountaineering Film Festival, 82
Kershaw, Phil, 100 sponsored climbs for Radio Lollipop, 120–33
Khyber Pass, 64, 65
Kikuli, Sherpa, 183
Kinshofer Route (K2), 183
Kirghiz people, 93–4, 104
Koksel Glacier, 96; Col, 100, 102–3, 152
Kongur, Mount, 19, 45, *see also* British Mount Kongur Expedition (1981); 144, 151, 168

Lancashire, Howard, 113, 159, 161, 165
Lane, Cass, 115, 118, 132, 137
La Tête d'Ane, 118
Le Pinnacle de l'Etacq, 116
Le Vyi, 116
Lewis, Pat, 20
Lister, Charles, 62, 110

Littlejohn, Pat, 118
Llanberis Pass, 40
Lliwedd, 31–4; Central Gully Direct,
 40–3
Llyn Llydaw, 32, 33
Llyn Ogwen, 25
Lundy, 112–14

MacInnes, Hamish, 56, 75–6
MacIntyre, Alex, 87
Main Wall, Avon Gorge, 30
Malbogies, 119, 132
Mallory, George, 24, 31, 177
Masherbrum, 60, 138
Maskrey, Andy, 143–6, 148–9, 152–8,
 182
Maskrey, Chepi, 146–8, 149, 152–4,
 158
Matterhorn, 73, 85, 108
McMullan, Ian, 161, 163, 165, 167–8,
 170–4
McNaught-Davies, Ian, 39, 50, 138
Messner, Gunther, 183
Messner, Reinhold, 183
Miller, David, 163, 167, 175
Minks, Pete, 37
Moffat, Gerry, 19
Molenaar, Dee, 183
Mont Blanc, 29
Montenevers, 28
Monzino Ridge, 182
Moralis, César, 146
Mortimer, Mike, 161–2, 166
Mount Everest Foundation, 145
Mountain magazine, 92
Mullach Bi, 166
Mummery, A. F., 183; Mummery Rib
 (K2), 183
Murison, Neil, 83; Radio Lollipop
 support, 121, 123, 126, 130–3
Murison, Sheila, 120
Murray, W. H., 106
Mustagh Tower, 59, 60
Muztagh Ata, 93
Myhill, Keith, 75

Naess, Arne, 171
Nanda Devi, 182
Nanga Parbat, 21, 181, 182–3
Newbigging, Carolyn, 90, 96

Newbigging, David, 90
Noel, Captain John, 23
Noyce, Wilfrid, 73
Nunn, Hilary, 137
Nunn, Paul, 20; first meeting, 37–8;
 1977 Expedition to Barnaj II, 63,
 67–70, 72; The Bat, 74–5, 77, 112,
 121, 123–7, 129; Radio Lollipop
 support, 123–7, 129–30, 145, 180

Oakley, Chris, 28
Odell, Noel, 182
Ogre, The, 63, 147
Ogwen, 25
Oiseval, 164, 167
Old Man of Hoy, 39, 120, 122–6,
 156
Old Man of Stoer, 124
Oswald, Mick, 24–5
Oswald, Richard, 24
Out With the Boys Again, Mountain
 magazine (Mike Thompson), 92

Palomani Grande, Expedition 1985;
 Base Camp, 149; Advance Base, 150;
 exploration of West Ridge, 152–3;
 reaching East Ridge, 155–6; summit,
 156
Palomani Tranca, 144, 149–51
Parson's Nose, 131
Patey, Tom, 39, 122
Peak District, 31, 34, 35
Pen-y-Pass, 33, 42
Porter, John, 118
Potts, Dave, 36, 50, 71
Prior, Ron, 113
Pyrenees, 28, 30

Rakaposhi, Mount, 21
Ramsay, Hilary, 110, 115
Rawalpindi, 22
Richardson, Laraine, 75, 82–3, 85,
 112
Richardson, Mike, 20, 112, 180
Riley, Tony, first meeting, 37;
 character, 39; filming A Great Effort,
 39, 51; 1976 Trango Expedition, 57,
 59–60, 72; The Bat, 74–82
Roaches, The, 130
Rongbuk Monastery, 176

Rouse, Al, 19, 20, 54, 74–5, 84; early climbing career, 84–5; friendship with Curran, 85; 1981 Expedition to West Ridge, Everest, 85; 1981 British Mount Kongur Expedition, 85, 89–97, 98–109, 110, 115–18, 144; British Fullers Expedition to K2 (1986), death, 160, 166, 181
Rowland, Clive, 64
Royal Geographical Society, 88, 144

Sabir, Nazir, 139
Scafell, 120; Central Buttress, 128, 129
Scott, Doug, 48, 64, 70, 75, 87, 138, 147
Senior Citizens, 118
Shepherds Crag, 128
Shipton, Eric, 50, 91
Shroud, 128
Simpson, Joe, 147, 180
Skye, 28
Slieve League, 164
Sloth, 130
Smith, Geoff, 1977 Barnaj II Expedition, 67–70
Smith, Ian, 20, 115–16
Smith, Robin, 73, 75
Smith, Rosie, 20
Smith, Viv, 115
Snowdon, 25; Snowdon Horseshoe, 31, 34, 120, 131, 176
South Col (Wilfrid Noyce), 24, 107
Stac an Armin, 162
Stac Biorach, 168, 171
Stac Lee, 162
Stanage Edge, 35, 129–30
St Kilda, 19, 159–69
Stobart, Tom, 23
Stokes, Brummie, 176

Tasker, Joe, 19, 20, 60, 85; climbing career, 85–7; British Mount Kongur Expedition (1981), 91–2, 95, 100–9; death, 110–11, 176
Taylor, Harry, 177
Tax Exile, 118
Terray, Lionel, 143
Thatcher, Denis, 89
Thexton, Pete, 113, 138

Thompson, Mike, 54, 92
Tier, Geoff, 1977 Barnaj II Expedition, 63–4, 69–72; 1985 Palomani Grande Expedition, 143–57
Tilman, W. H., 182
Toogood, Bob, 63–4, 114–15
Trango Tower, 19, 50–3; 1975 Expedition (Mo Anthoine), 51; 1976 Trango Tower Expedition, 51–61; first view, 52–3; Base Camp, 53; Advance Base, 57; summit, 60; 63, 68, 71, 144, 158
Trento Film Festival, 85, 87
Tryfan, 25

Uli Biaho, 50
Untrodden Andes, The (C. G. Egeler and T. de Booy), 143
Upon That Mountain (Eric Shipton), 50
Upper Nantillons Glacier, 30

Walters, Rick, 69
Ward, Dr Michael, 84, 88, 92, 95, 105–9
Watkins, Michael, 26, 179
Wen Zawn, 139
Wharncliffe Crags, 34, 37
Whillance, Peter, 19, 160–1, 163, 165, 168, 170–4
Whillans, Don, 20, 28; and Joe Brown, 55, 76, 83; character, 134; in Cornwall, 134–8; BMC Conference, 139; A Dream of White Horses, 139–41, 142, 145; death, 158
White, Caroline, 112
Whybrow, Barry, 71
Williams, Edward, 102
Wilson, David, 88; British Mount Kongur Expedition (1981), 98–100, 103–5, 109
Wilson, Ken, 118, 129
Windgather, 130
Winthrop Young, Geoffrey, 31
Wintringham, Ben, 118
Wintringham, Marion, 118
Wolf, 'Mrufka', 181
Wolfe, Dudley, 183

Yates, John, 72
Yates, Simon, 147

(*Index compiled by Gemma Curran*)